Critical Analysis in Psychology

T0349992

Critical Analysis in Psychology

The essential guide to interrogating published research

A.J. Shepherd

Open University Press

Open University Press
McGraw Hill
Unit 4,
Foundation Park
Roxborough Way
Maidenhead
SL6 3UD

email: emea_uk_ireland@mheducation.com
world wide web: www.openup.co.uk

First edition published 2022

Figures 3.1, 3.2, 3.3, 3.4 and 3.5 Reprinted from Frontiers in Psychology, 8, Yeh, Su-Ling, Lane, Timothy Joseph, Chang, An-Yi and Chien, Sung-En, Switching to the Rubber Hand, (2017), with permission from Yeh, Lane, Chang and Chien, https://creativecommons.org/licenses/by/4.0/

A catalogue record of this book is available from the British Library

ISBN-13: 9780335249893
ISBN-10: 0335249892
eISBN: 9780335249909

Library of Congress Cataloging-in-Publication Data
CIP data applied for

Typeset by Transforma Pvt. Ltd., Chennai, India

Praise page

"This book is the fruit of Alex Shepherd's remarkable teaching experience in one of the most prestigious universities in the world. She designed and led a highly successful course on Critical Analysis, which has been running for more than a decade.

Alex has provided students with a formidable tool to understand and constructively critique published research covering a vast variety of methods.

This publication will certainly become the main reference for science students at BSc, MSc and PhD levels."

Roberto Filippi, PhD, University College London

"I highly recommend this book as essential reading for psychology students at all levels from undergraduate to PhD. It provides a friendly and engaging guide to developing critical evaluation skills through the use of clear and accessible examples that capture the reader's interest."

Dr Elisa Lewis, Senior Lecturer, London South Bank University

"With unchallenged research output being shared more and more in the public domain, this book should be required reading, not only for its target student audience but also for intelligent and curious non-experts. Alex Shepherd offers an accessible forensic filleting of published research articles, with helpful how-to guides showing what questions to ask and (more importantly) what the answers mean."

Gina Rippon, Professor Emeritus of Cognitive Neuroimaging,
Author of The Gendered Brain

Contents

Foreword

A proper education in Psychology includes an understanding of the various types of research that constitute psychological knowledge. Carrying out practical work is one way in which students can gain such understanding, while reading published research is another. This book aims to help students adopt a critical approach to research publications. It captures the excitement of research and takes students through the tried-and-tested aspects of the Critical Analysis course built up over several decades at Birkbeck, University of London. Alex Shepherd, with her own impressive publications in both visual perception and migraine, has contributed to that development, and her success in teaching the course is apparent in this unique, helpful and appealing book.

Dr Vernon Gregg
Associate Research Fellow
Birkbeck College, University of London

Acknowledgements

I would like to thank everyone who has made this book possible. Teaching assistants and students have asked me repeatedly to write it, and so I have. Foremost, I thank all my teaching assistants over the years who have led the small group discussions during the class sessions. There have been many, and I always smile whenever I see them now in faculty positions across the United Kingdom and abroad. The same can be said for some of my students. I would particularly like to thank Jo Kenrick, Kaili Rimfeld and James Vance, who have been with me and this course for many years. All were previous students who stayed on as my teaching assistants.

I'd also like to thank Dr Paul Barber, from whom I inherited this course on his retirement nearly two decades ago and Dr Vernon Gregg, for his encouragement over the years. Dr Virginia Eatough contributed to the discussion of qualitative research in Chapter 9. Thanks too to Michael Leunig who allowed me to reproduce two of his cartoons: he has been one of my favourite cartoonists since I was an undergraduate and the content is so apposite. Finally, I thank all my students over the years who have kept me on my toes and, in particular, Aidan Chappell, who agreed to let me reproduce some of his work in Chapter 8.

1 Introduction: why you need to read this book

Many books on research methodology and analysis describe issues and procedures and then provide short examples of this or that issue or procedure, often taken from published research articles, but presented as a snippet and out of context from the complete article. This book, instead, turns the organisation of the material around. It starts by presenting, in detail, complete published research articles and then walks you through them, identifying the issues raised in each section of each article. You can be told, by your lecturers or tutors, to think about this, think about that, but sometimes until you are led by the hand and shown how to do the thinking about this or that in the context of a complete research article, you can get lost – which doesn't help to build your confidence. Often it just alienates you. Consequently, the principal aims of this book are to:

1 encourage critical reading and analysis of psychological research articles;
2 show how design principles and statistics are applied in psychological research;
3 consider the psychological importance of published research articles.

This book is aimed primarily at later year undergraduate students, masters' students and doctoral students in psychology. It should be accessible to science students in related disciplines and to others with an interest in psychological science. It provides a consolidation of material on research methods typically covered in the first year or two of an undergraduate degree in psychology. There is a change in emphasis from the way research methods and statistics are usually taught in the early years of an undergraduate degree, which tends to focus on how to do them. The switch in emphasis in this book is its focus on how to use and evaluate research rather than how to do it. In other words, this book is definitely not a how-to-do book on statistical and research methods. Statistical and research methods do need to be discussed, but they are covered only in the context of the techniques used in a particular journal article and whether their use was appropriate.

The focus of this book is on *critical evaluation*, not just criticism (it is often easy to criticise but there must be strengths as well or the article would not have made it through the review process and been published). Both strengths and weaknesses ought to be considered when you read an article. Sometimes you also need to place the work in its historical context: when and where it was published; whether it addresses a new area of research or whether it sits amongst dozens, hundreds or even more articles on a similar topic.

In more detail, this book will guide you through these different issues in each chapter so that, by the end, you will be able to:

- review research articles comprehensively, critically and objectively;
- assess the soundness of experimental designs, the methods and the statistical treatments used in actual research studies;
- interpret the results of a study and assess the adequacy of the conclusions drawn (are they justified?);
- propose solutions to the shortcomings of particular research reports;
- acknowledge the strengths of particular reports;
- appreciate ethical and practical constraints when setting up a research question;
- write a stand-alone critique of a research article;
- frame comments on each article realistically, taking into account the publication process (peer review, remit, length, succinctness) and when and where the study was conducted.

Throughout, there is an emphasis on linking sections, considering the article *as a whole* so that, for example, the method and variables selected are related back to the hypotheses, the analyses performed are related back to the method, selected variables and hypotheses, and the conclusions drawn are related back to all four. The style and content of the book are intended to make reading of articles more engaging, light-hearted and accessible than books that present a discussion of issues in research with few complete examples. If you engage with this book, it will provide you with skills transferable to other courses and further study.

This book has evolved from a course on Critical Analysis that I have taught for nearly twenty years after inheriting it on a colleague's retirement (see Barber, 2002, 2004). The articles selected cover a range of topics, methods and analyses within experimental psychology. From student comments, the course has enabled them to be active – rather than passive – readers of scientific articles. It made them feel less like a student and more like a researcher. It also gave them a new insight into published research articles, the publishing process, and an understanding of the responsibility that researchers carry when they write up and publish their findings. They felt they were confident to be able to critically evaluate written information, whether it be a research article or something in a magazine or newspaper, rather than simply accept the claims made because the work has been published. Finally, they thought that it also made them more critical of their own research and hence they produced better work themselves.

Each chapter is devoted to different themes. Two learning aids are described in Chapters 2 and 6, which can be applied to all research articles in Experimental

Psychology. The first of these learning aids is the ten general questions (10GQ, Chapter 2), which ensure every aspect of an article is considered and they give you the factual foundation for a critique. The second is a mnemonic using the anagram JARGON? to help in the selection of issues to include in a standalone critique, both positive and negative (Chapter 6). These learning aids are not presented as recipes; rather, they are tools to help you identify the strengths and weaknesses in published research articles, prioritise them, and construct an overall critical assessment. This is a crucial difference to other texts in this area: those that do offer critiques of articles provide comments relevant to that particular article, they do not provide an overarching framework that can be applied to any research article. They can leave you with a blank slate as you approach each new article to review, which can be daunting. The 10GQ and JARGON? rubrics set the scene, giving you a place to start.

This is not a 'what is science?' book, so it does not include a discussion of different, broad approaches to science. It is a 'here is some published science, let's take a look at it and evaluate' book. It includes experimental research, predominantly (but not exclusively) lab-based, yet the discussion of issues raised on justification, method and design are equally applicable to electrophysiological (EEG, ERP) and imaging (fMRI, MEG) research,[1] as studies using these techniques begin with the design of an experiment to be completed while participants are being recorded or scanned. Detailed discussion of the analyses of electrophysiological or scanning data is not, however, included. It also does not cover in detail qualitative research, yet most of the components of JARGON? and some of the 10GQs are applicable to qualitative research as well. A discussion of aspects of these methods that are in common is provided in Chapter 9.

As mentioned, the 10GQs ensure you consider every aspect of a research article and give you the factual foundation for a critique. The JARGON? scheme has been constructed to help if you are to write up your thoughts for someone else to read. The scheme encourages you to select and prioritise issues that are worth including in a critique, either positive or negative. Your critique should be written with the reader you have in mind. It should not be a mind dump of everything you have to say about an article, it should be carefully constructed and probably will not include more than five to seven issues with a particular article. The precise number of issues will, of course, depend on the article at hand. When writing a critique, you are often told to write it for 'the intelligent non-expert who has not read the paper'. What does that mean? I always suggest you should write your critique as if explaining the article to a friend. You should provide enough detail so that they can decide if it is worth reading the article for themselves. Therefore, you have to provide a complete account of what has been done and highlight both strengths and weaknesses of the article as a whole.

Chapters 3–5 and 7–8 discuss actual research articles. You will get the most out of this book if you obtain copies of these articles: you should be able to find them through your university or college library, and then read them for yourself first, before reading how they are discussed in this book. One of the articles is open access, so freely available to anyone with an internet connection. For those who cannot access the articles from your university, college or library, a detailed synopsis of each article is provided at the start of each chapter (which you can critique).

When reading articles, be mindful that they have been peer-reviewed by at least two other people. Sometimes the reviewers disagree with each other and the author has to perform a juggling act to revise their paper and keep both reviewers happy. Journal editors should step in to help resolve differences in opinion between reviewers, but sometimes they do not. Most journals operate a 'blind' peer review, that is, the author of the submitted article does not know who is reviewing their paper (although they can sometimes guess). Reviewers are people, with their own agendas, and some hide behind anonymity and are possibly less polite than they would be if they had to put their name at the end of their review. They can force authors to include things they may not want to. Keep this in mind when you are reading an article if the content seems to drift off into another topic in a slightly disjointed way with several citations to one person's work: it may be a clue that a reviewer insisted their work be included rather than a flaw in the logic of the author. Or, it could be a flaw in the logic of the author! Also keep in mind that the pressure to publish in a timely way can lead to less rigorous research than is ideal, particularly if the research is on a new and emerging topic. New topics tend to produce greater variation in the quality of research produced, as people want to get their thoughts out there, fast, before others do anything similar. Most research is well motivated, and it is always easy to criticise with 20:20 hindsight, but remember that the review process may force the author to include tangential themes. Reflect on the ultimate outcome of any research article, whatever its strengths and weaknesses: all in all, has it contributed to your understanding of the topic?

Before getting to the chapters, here are a few questions and tips to get started. First, it is always a good idea to imagine yourself being a participant in the experiment(s): what would you feel like if you were asked to do what is described? Would you feel self-conscious? Would you prefer not to comply? Would you be wondering what it was all about and do you think it would be easy to guess what it was all about? How long does the experiment take? Would you get bored or tired? Are you alone in a room or are multiple people being tested at the same time? Is the experimenter in the room watching you? Would that make a difference, particularly if it is just you and the experimenter in a room or laboratory? What if the experimenter is your lecturer or tutor, would that change how you behaved? Are you being paid or are you a student participating for course credit? Would that make a difference?

Also think about the conduct and presentation of the research and the treatment of the participants. Whether or not there is anything unpleasant about what participants are being asked to do, have the authors discussed any ethical issues the study may raise? Has an ethics committee approved their research? This is essential for all research studies in Psychology. Have the authors taken care to ensure that their participants will not be distressed or made to feel uncomfortable? Are you convinced the participants have been told enough about the study before they start so that they are able to consent to take part? Do they understand that they can withdraw from the study at any time and ask for their data to be removed up until the point of publication? Have they been assured of anonymity? Was written informed consent obtained? Were they given the courtesy of a debrief, having completed the study?

When you read an article, read it through once, fairly quickly, to orient yourself to the scope and content of the article. As you read it, jot things down in the margins like 'hypothesis', 'independent variable', 'dependent variable', 'procedure', 'design', etc. This makes it easy for you to find the information you need for the 10GQ. Jot down thoughts that occur to you as well, as they may be relevant for your general critique when you come to write one. Highlight parts of the text that are not clear on the first reading rather than dwell on them. You can go back to these sections after you have read the whole report and give them more time. You can then work out if the lack of clarity is in your lack of understanding or is in the author's exposition. (You should not always assume it is your understanding!) Then read the whole report again and have a go at the 10GQ.

In summary: why do you need to read this book? It is a good idea to do Critical Analysis and apply it to anything you read or listen to – articles, books, on-line reports, newspaper articles, TV or public presentations and radio interviews. Additionally, when you do your own research, you must think about the design, conduct, analysis, interpretation and presentation of your work. This book will help you with your own research and/or any literature reviews you need to do.

Note

1 Common electrophysiological measures include electroencephalography (EEG), evoked potentials (EP) and event-related potentials (ERP). Imaging techniques include functional magnetic resonance imaging (fMRI) and magnetoencephalography (MEG).

References

Barber, P. (2002). Critical analysis of psychological research: Rationale and design for a proposed course for the undergraduate psychology curriculum. *Psychology Learning & Teaching*, 2(2), 95–101. https://doi.org/10.2304/plat.2002.2.2.95.

Barber, P. (2004). Critical analysis of psychological research II: Delivering a course for inclusion in the core curriculum for Psychology. *Psychology Learning & Teaching*, 3(1), 15–26. https://doi.org/10.2304/plat.2003.3.1.15.

2　The ten general questions

The ten general questions (10GQs) ask you to consider each section of a journal article, including the study's justification and the chosen experimental design; whether the design is appropriate; the clarity of the written exposition; the analyses and conclusions that are drawn; the logic that flows through the different sections. They ask you to decide what the authors wanted to examine and assess how they have chosen to do so, and whether they have constrained in some way the conclusions that they are able to draw. The questions are applicable to any experimental research study. To fully answer these questions, it is useful to refresh your understanding of the following terms:

Descriptive statistics

- levels of measurement (nominal/categorical, ordinal, interval and ratio);
- measures of central tendency (mode, median, mean);
- measures of dispersion/variability (the range, interquartile range, variance, standard deviation and standard error);
- appropriate ways to represent data graphically and in summary tables.

Inferential statistics

- chi-square;
- two group comparisons – nonparametric and parametric [Wilcoxon matched-pairs signed ranks test, Wilcoxon rank-sum/Mann-Whitney U-test, Sign Test, t-tests (related/paired-sample and unrelated/independent samples)];
- correlation – non-parametric and parametric;
- Z-scores;
- ANOVA and non-parametric alternatives;
- regression;
- factor and principal components analyses.

Experimental designs

- variables (dependent, independent, manipulated, controlled, nuisance, confounding);
- conceptual and operational definitions of variables;

- designs (within-subjects, between-subjects, mixed, quasi-experimental, correlational);
- strengths and weaknesses of different experimental designs;
- appropriate statistical techniques for each type of experimental design;
- internal and external validity.

The ten general questions, 10GQs (basic factual questions about any experimental article)

1 (a) Does the report specify an hypothesis? If so, what is it? Is there more than one? (b) What background or rationale is provided as justification for any hypothesis?

2 (a) Specify all the variables in the investigation and indicate what sort of variables they are (e.g. dependent vs. independent, manipulated, controlled, nuisance, confounding). Specify what level of measurement has been achieved for each dependent variable (nominal, ordinal, interval, ratio). (b) Do the selected variables address the research hypothesis/hypotheses?

3 What did the participants have to do? (briefly) Is the study easily replicable?

4 (a) What experimental design was used? (b) Do the method and design address the research hypothesis/hypotheses?

5 What comparisons were chosen for statistical analysis?

6 What analysis was used? Was it appropriate?

7 What was the main result?

8 What conclusions were drawn? Were they valid?

9 What are your main criticisms of the report?

10 What are the main strengths of the report?

Notes on the 10GQs

1(a). Does the report specify an hypothesis? If so, what is it? Is there more than one? A hypothesis is a specific prediction about the outcome of the study. The answer to this question will always be 'yes': the research would not be completed if the authors were not interested in testing at least one idea. Sometimes the hypotheses are clearly stated in the article's Introduction, usually at the end but, if they are not clearly stated, they will need to be dug out from the background information, previous cited work and the analyses performed.

You should unearth however many hypotheses the authors have by looking at the Introduction and by checking how many analyses have been performed. There will be an hypothesis for each analysis, indeed, that is why statistical testing is referred to as hypothesis testing.

Once you have identified the hypothesis or hypotheses, work out whether they are directional (the authors predict how they think the data will come out) or bi-directional (they just think there will a difference).

1(b). What background or rationale is provided as justification for any hypothesis? All hypotheses should be grounded in prior research or theory – preferably both. The authors should make it clear how their research builds on what has gone before. The authors should instil confidence that they know sufficient relevant literature. You should be able to understand why they are telling you each piece of prior research or theory.

2(a). Specify all the variables in the investigation and indicate what sort of variables they are (e.g. dependent vs. independent, manipulated, controlled, nuisance, confounding). Specify what level of measurement has been achieved for each dependent variable (nominal, ordinal, interval, ratio). The classic confusion is between dependent and independent variables. Dependent variables are the data (hint: both words begin with 'D'). Independent variables are those variables that I, as the experimenter, have chosen to select (hint: both words begin with 'I').

Controlled variables are those I control, as the name implies: for example, I may choose to match up the age and gender of each participant in two different groups. Or I may test each participant at the same time of day and ask them not to have had coffee or tea for an hour before the test session. I may want to test their visual acuity and select only those with 20:20 or 20:25 vision[1] so as to be sure that all the participants can see adequately. Age, gender, time of day, caffeine intake and visual acuity would be controlled variables.

Nuisance variables are those that may have an effect on a person's performance, but are unlikely to have systematic effects on the performance of the different groups that the author plans to compare. How hungry a participant is, for example, may affect concentration, but it is unlikely to be the case that everyone in one group is hungrier than everyone in the other group. Confounding variables, on the other hand, are variables that do differ systematically between the groups. If there is a confound, the author cannot be sure that any group differences are due to what has been set up in the experiment, the independent/manipulated variable, or whether the group differences can be attributed to the confounding variable.

Another important distinction is between the concept underlying a study and how it has been operationalised. For example, if an experimenter wants to study young children's perception of danger, they will need independent and dependent variables that capture some aspect of young children's grasp of the concept of danger. It is a laudable area of study, but how to carry it out? It would not be ethical to put young children in various dangerous situations and just see what happens, so the experimenter is immediately constrained. In one study, the authors chose to use cards with line drawings depicting potentially dangerous and non-dangerous situations. Children of various ages (age group was the independent variable) were asked to identify the dangerous situations by sorting them into two piles, dangerous and non-dangerous (the dependent variable: how many dangers were successfully identified). In a second experiment, they were asked to recognise the dangerous situation from a set of four cards (the dependent variable: how many dangers were successfully recognised). The authors chose to operationalise the concept of danger using a card sorting and a card identification task (Grieve & Williams, 1985). Here ask yourself: how close together are the concept they wanted to study and the way they chose to study it? That is, how close are the conceptual and operational definitions of the variables?

Levels of measurement refer to the data. The four are nominal/categorical, ordinal, interval and ratio. Nominal/categorical data are frequencies: the experiment usually has a limited number of categories and the experimenter counts up how many of the participants belong to each category. For example, participants could be given a simple question such as 'the prime minister tells the truth' and the participants could be given the option of saying 'yes', 'no' or 'do not know'. The researcher may be interested in the responses of younger and older people, so would select a cut-off between young and old (perhaps 40 years of age) and then count how many younger and older people endorsed 'yes', 'no' or 'do not know'. These would be nominal/categorical data.

Ordinal data can be put in a simple order, or a simple scale, yet the difference between scale points 1 and 2 is not the same as the difference between scale points 2 and 3. Many rating scales yield ordinal data: for example, if participants rate their mood on a 7-point scale ranging from 'happy' (scale point 1) to 'sad' (scale point 7), you cannot know that the difference in mood between scale points 1 and 2 means the same thing as the difference in mood between scale points 6 and 7, nor if the midpoint means 'neither happy nor sad', or whether it perhaps means 'a little bit happy and a little bit sad'. You could ask yourself whether there are as many gradations of happiness as there are levels of sadness? If the answer is 'no', you have collected ordinal data.

A really poor use of rating scales is to use ones that simply consist of a 10 cm line, with two opposing adjectives at either end (such as happy and sad), and to ask participants to place a mark somewhere along the line to express their state of mind. Some people use these and then measure, in millimetres, where the tick mark is on the line for each scale and each participant. These data are pretty much useless: it is just not sensible to consider a tick mark placed at 6.5 cm along the line as meaningfully different from a tick mark placed at 6.6 cm. Fortunately, this type of scale is not used very much these days; people tend to use scales with discrete boxes or numbers that participants must endorse rather than continuous 10 cm lines.

Interval data often also come from (better constructed) rating scales, also referred to as Likert scales. This time the differences between scale points are the same along the scale, but there is no true zero: zero does not indicate the absence of the thing being measured. The classic example is temperature: zero does not mean the absence of temperature, it refers to a decidedly cool one. When the end-points of rating scales are better opposites, such as having a 7-point scale with the end-points 'agree' (scale point +3) and 'disagree' (scale point –3), and the authors instruct their participants to use the scale with equal intervals, then the data can be considered interval (although hardliners would insist they are still ordinal). Scale point zero can also be considered to be 'neither agree nor disagree'. The consistency or use of the scale across people is more comparable if the participants are told to use the scale in that way. The most useful scales use an odd number of scale points, so there is a midpoint and no more than seven or nine scale points. Beyond that, their use becomes unwieldly, as it could be questioned whether people can make such fine discriminations between scale points.

The final type of data, ratio data, is an interval scale that does have a true zero. Time is a classic example: zero seconds means the absence of time. You can also meaningfully talk about multiples: 10 seconds is meaningfully twice as long as 5 seconds.

2(b). Do the selected variables address the research hypothesis/ hypotheses? This question is best discussed in the context of actual examples; see Chapters 3 to 5.

3. What did the participants have to do? (briefly) Is the study easily replicable? Here it helps to imagine yourself being a participant in the experiment. Summarise what the authors did and jot down comments about what you would have thought about when doing it. This section does not have to be long; write it as a reminder for yourself, and consider whether boredom, tiredness or even embarrassment might be involved.

To answer if it is replicable, look closely at the method, who was tested, what equipment was used and whether any of the tasks were standard tests or made specifically for the experiment. If patient groups are involved, do they mention who made the diagnosis? If the experiment involved visual tests, did they test their eyesight? If there are cognitive tests, do they consider matching participants on a measure of IQ or educational level? It is not uncommon for participants to be students who receive course credits for their time, whereas if members of the public are tested, they are usually given a small honorarium. Consider whether that may affect the motivation of those being tested.

Look also at what the experimenter was doing: what instructions were used? Was there any indication that the experimenter provided leading instructions? Was the experimenter known to the participants? Would that affect your performance? Finally, have the authors discussed ethics and whether there was a debriefing at the end of the test session?

4(a). What experimental design was used? There are various types of experimental designs. In true experimental designs, participants are randomly allocated to the different conditions. If there are two groups comprised of randomly allocated participants, it is a between-subjects design. If there is one group performing more than one task, it is a within-subjects design. If there are two groups of randomly allocated participants performing more than one task, it is a mixed design (both between-subjects and within-subjects). When people cannot be randomly allocated to groups, as in a clinical group comparison, the design is between-subjects and quasi-experimental. Correlational designs do not use group comparisons, rather two or more measures are taken from each participant (a within-subjects design) to determine whether there are any relationships between the measures.

4(b). Do the method and design address the research hypothesis/ hypotheses? This question is best discussed in the context of actual examples; see Chapters 3 to 5.

5. What comparisons were chosen for statistical analysis? This question is again designed to help you extract the important comparisons and your answer can be quite short. You can present the analysis/analyses in a summary table, a tree diagram, or just list the comparisons in a sentence or two or, if longer, as bullet point notes. A summary table or list is easier to refer to if you need to check what the authors have done, rather than re-reading the text.

6. What analysis was used? Was it appropriate? Again, the answer to this question can be quite short (depending on how many analyses were performed). See the list of inferential statistics above you are likely to come across in research articles in Psychology.

Most statistical tests require the data to meet some assumptions. Parametric tests typically require that the data are measured at the interval or ratio level, that the data are normally distributed and that there is homogeneity of variance. Kolmogorov-Smirnov tests can be used to assess if the data from each sample come from a specific distribution, including the normal distribution (for a review of alternative tests, see Ghasemi & Zahediasl, 2012). Levene's test can be used to test if two or more samples have equivalent variances. General guidance is that the variance of the largest sample should not be three times greater than the variance of the smallest. This can usually be worked out from data reported in tables or figures.

Non-parametric tests can be used when all of the assumptions required for parametric tests have not been met. You should still check what assumptions the non-parametric tests require, however.

7. What was the main result? Before reading what the authors pick up on and present as the main result, it is a good idea to look at the data presented yourself, whether in a graph, a table or in the text, and decide for yourself what differences, if any, jump out at you. Then read the author's account and see if it concurs with your appraisal of the data.

8. What conclusions were drawn? Were they valid? This can be quite a fun question to answer: do the analyses performed map onto the conclusions that were drawn? Have they correctly identified any differences between groups or between conditions? Do their conclusions tie in with the original hypotheses? In other words, have the hypotheses been adequately tested?

9. What are your main criticisms of the report? This one is really up to you as the reader, but note the word 'main'. Quibbling over the sample size is unlikely to be a main criticism whereas drawing conclusions that are unwarranted probably is. Look out for over-speculation as well: sometimes the conclusions drawn can go far beyond what is warranted from one modest study.

In this section you could also consider the internal and external validity of the study. There are many ways internal validity can be compromised, some of which can be eliminated with careful planning. For example, participants should be randomly allocated to the conditions in a true experiment so that all the little personal differences they bring along with them, as they are all different people, do not have a systematic effect on the comparison of experimental conditions. Other factors that affect internal validity cannot be eliminated (e.g. boredom or fatigue), so there are procedures to ensure that they do not have any systematic effect on the data collected. For example, when there are multiple tasks, ideally they should be presented in a counterbalanced order, if there are enough trials to allow complete counterbalancing. If there are fewer trials, then they should be presented in a random order. This ensures that boredom or fatigue, which cannot be eliminated, does not have a systematic effect on the comparisons.

A common limitation that affects external validity stems from the sample recruited. As far as possible, participants should be randomly selected from the population the researchers are interested in generalising their results to. This ensures the sample tested is representative of that population. Often, however, all the participants are students participating for course credit: they will probably have a limited age range, there may be a gender bias, and their motivation may differ to people who are given an honorarium for their time. This limits how generalisable the results are to the wider population.

If participants can guess what the experiment is about – that is, if the experiment has demand characteristics – there can be various consequences, each of which will compromise the internal and external validity of a study. Some participants may try to behave as they think is expected, trying to provide 'correct' responses. Others, the Machiavellians, may try to thwart or undermine the study by doing the opposite of what they think the experimenter is after. Others may try to remain impervious but, in the act of trying to ignore what they think is the aim of the study, they no longer behave as they normally would. Sometimes a social desirability questionnaire is included to try to assess whether a person likes to give socially desirable answers (see, for example, Crowne & Marlowe, 1960). If they do, then the reliability of their data from the experiment can be considered dubious.

10. What are the main strengths of the report? As for Question 9, this one is really up to you. It is always easy to criticise with hindsight, but your critique of a paper should be balanced: you should be able to find something positive to say. It could be a new area, a clever task, a new twist to an old question or an impeccable design and conduct.

Note

1 An acuity of 20:20 indicates that a person can see, at 20 feet, the same small letters on an eye chart that an average healthy eye can see at 20 feet. 20:25 indicates that a person can see, at 20 feet, the letters on an eye chart that an average healthy eye can see if it had moved back to 25 feet. Acuities of 6:6 and 6:9 are the same, except that distance is expressed in metres.

References

Crowne, D. P., & Marlowe, D. (1960). A new scale of social desirability independent of psychopathology. *Journal of Consulting Psychology, 24*(4), 349–354. https://doi.org/10.1037/h0047358.

Ghasemi, A., & Zahediasl, S. (2012). Normality tests for statistical analysis: A guide for non-statisticians. *International Journal of Endocrinology and Metabolism, 10*(2), 486–489. https://doi.org/10.5812/ijem.3505.

Grieve, R., & Williams, A. (1985). Young children's perception of danger. *British Journal of Developmental Psychology, 3*(4), 385–392. https://doi.org/10.1111/j.2044-835X.1985.tb00990.x.

3 Action perception, imitation and illusions

In this chapter, we will discuss two articles that share common themes and raise similar issues. Their topic is, broadly, imitation and illusion. Issues raised include internal validity (confounds, demand characteristics) and external validity (who has been tested, whether the tasks selected are natural). Further limitations include the possibility of making inferences about the underlying neural function of brain areas involved when performing a task from behavioural studies. Data from purely behavioural studies cannot provide evidence for or against models of the underlying neural circuitry, so appeals need to be made to other studies with different methodologies. The authors of these two papers do want to explain their data in neuroscientific terms, so you should consider how well the methodologies from different types of research marry together and, therefore, how firm or speculative the basis for the work is as well as how plausible the conclusions that are drawn are.

> *Recap: Internal validity* refers to the conduct of the experiment, that is, how well the research has been carried out. *External validity* refers to how far any results can be generalised beyond the particular participants who have been recruited.

Yeh, S.-L., Lane, T.J., Chang, A.-Y., & Chien, S.-E. (2017). Switching to the rubber hand. *Frontiers in Psychology, 8,* 2172. https://doi.org/10.3389/fpsyg.2017.02172.

This article is an open access publication.

Many of you will have heard of the phantom limb phenomenon, where people who have had a limb amputated can still feel an itch on the skin or pain in the missing part. You may also know that the brain shows plasticity, whereby those areas that are no longer receiving input – because the limb is missing – are recruited by nearby areas, resulting in remapping of the missing limb onto different body regions, usually near to the missing limb. 'Near' should be construed with reference to the somatosensory cortex homunculus. The representation of the body is mapped across the surface of the primary somatosensory cortex in an orderly fashion: if you traverse the surface from the outside edge of the postcentral gyrus in the parietal lobe to the midline, you find areas devoted to the face, then the fingers, hand, arm, torso, hip, upper leg, lower leg, foot, then toes. So, if the lower leg is amputated, patients may experience referred sensations on the upper leg. If a hand is amputated, they may experience sensations on the arm, or on the face. A curious feature is that, when this occurs, the itch can be relieved by scratching the remapped area.

Treating phantom pain is more difficult, but one approach when the missing body part is a hand, arm or leg is to create an illusion of the missing part using a mirror. If the patient positions themselves so that the existing part of the hand, arm or leg and the missing part are on the far side of the mirror and the intact limb is by the reflective side, the mirror can be positioned so that when the patient looks at the intact limb and its reflection in the mirror, it looks like they have two intact limbs. If they move the intact limb, the image seen in the mirror necessarily moves, and patients have reported that it feels like the missing limb is moving (Ramachandran & Rodgers-Ramachandran, 1996; for a more recent review, see Guenther, 2016). With repeated training sessions using the mirror, long-term phantom pain can be reduced. The efficacy of mirror therapy has been attributed to reducing conflict between visual feedback and the proprioceptive representation of the missing limb, or to the activation of mirror neurons in the contralateral somatosensory cortex (Chan et al., 2007).

Recently, researchers have asked: if amputees can imagine a phantom limb, can everyone? The answer appears to be 'yes', inasmuch as people can experience body transfer illusions, where they embody limbs that are not their own. Since it was first highlighted, there have been thousands of reports that observers can experience a rubber hand as their own: the rubber hand illusion (RHI) (Botvinick & Cohen, 1998). In the classic example, the participant places one hand on a table in front of them, although it is occluded from their view (typically, it is placed on the far side of a partition, but it can also be inserted into a tube, or covered with a cloth) and, in its place in front of them, is placed a rubber hand. The participant looks at the rubber hand. If both the rubber hand and the occluded hand are stroked in synchrony, after a while the participant begins to adopt the rubber hand as their own to such an extent that if the rubber hand is subsequently hit with a hammer, the participant will jump.[1]

Body transfer illusions are not restricted to the hands, as they can occur for other body parts, such as the feet or face (reviewed in Braun et al., 2018), although the RHI is by far the most well studied. Many of the explanations for these illusions refer to neural plasticity, cross-modal interactions, inter-modal correlations or intersensory biases, which are typically considered to be low-level processes. Different modalities refer to different senses, in this example, touch and sight. Low-level processes are those that are thought to involve early neural processing, typically automatic, which do not require active attention. For example, if I look out of the window and see something move, I am aware something has moved – low-level processing—but to identify what has moved, I will need to attend to it – higher-level processing). Yeh *et al.* (2017) looked at possible cognitive influences on the RHI using task-switching and mind-wandering paradigms. Task switching requires a person to shift attention between two or more tasks. Mind-wandering paradigms assess thoughts and feelings that can intrude when a person is engaged in an attentionally demanding task.

Synopsis

Introduction

Yeh *et al.* (2017) provide a historical review of the rubber hand illusion (RHI) and traditional explanations in terms of the integration and interaction of low-level processes (vision, touch, proprioception) from a body-centred frame of reference: people have a sense of where their body is in space and what they can see and feel. One explanation for the RHI is that the parts of the external world that are in the immediate vicinity of the person, the peripersonal, can also be experienced as belonging to the self.

Yeh and colleagues provide evidence for some cognitive intrusion in the RHI. Citing Tsakiris (2010, 2011, 2017), for example, they refer to Armel and Ramachandran (2003), who apparently reported that the fake object must look like a hand for the RHI to occur; Costantini and Haggard (2007), who apparently found that the rubber and (hidden) real hands must have similar postures; and Lloyd (2007), who found the RHI disappeared if the distance between the (hidden) real hand and the fake hand exceeded 30 cm.

In fact, Tsakiris (2010, 2011, 2017) and Armel and Ramachandran (2003) reported the opposite. In one experiment, Armel and Ramachandran induced the typical RHI. When one of the rubber hand's fingers was then bent backwards in a painful position, their participants flinched. They also measured skin conductance (SC) and found it increased when the rubber finger was bent backwards, a sign of autonomic nervous system arousal. Their participants also rated their ownership of the rubber hand on a scale from 1 (it felt nothing like their own hand) to 10 (it felt exactly like their own hand). Average ratings were over 7.

In a second experiment, they placed a plaster on the table and stroked the table synchronously with the hidden real hand. When they subsequently pulled the plaster part-way off the table, the participants again reacted as if they had embodied that part of the table, as indicated by ratings and a small increase in SC. Participants reported they had imagined a hand on or near the part of the table where the plaster was, so they had embodied part of a table! Neither illusion occurred when the strokes on the real and rubber hands were asynchronous.

Armel and Ramachandran (2003) also reported their participants experienced the RHI when the rubber hand was positioned 3 feet away.

This is a cautionary tale: you should never rely on secondary sources if you are going to quote someone's work – go back to the original work and read for yourself what was said and done. See also Paradis (2006) for a (humorous) review of errors some authors have made when citing prior research. (The article is on neurolinguistics, but you do not need to know anything about neurolinguistics to appreciate the issues he raises.)

Yeh *et al.* maintain that the possible effects of 'higher' cognitive functions have not been adequately assessed. They comment on variability in the experience of the RHI for different people, which they consider to be inconsistent with a multisensory integration or other simply low-level reports – if everyone has the same make-up, everyone should experience the illusion – so what accounts for variability including the absence of the illusion for up to one-third of people tested? Here they bring in the role of attention and its interplay with lower-level integrative processes. They cite several studies on the effect attention can have on multisensory integration, although the cited work does not involve the RHI or the sense of the body. This is the background to justify their study to explore whether executive functions can modulate the RHI. (Executive functions are cognitive processes that enable people to interact with their environment and attain their goals; they include attention, memory, flexible thinking, organisation and self-control.)

Yeh and colleagues chose mind wandering and task switching to assess executive control. They define mind wandering as a failure of executive control to block internal thoughts and feelings while attempting to perform external tasks. They define task switching as a component of executive control that enables people to switch attention from internal to external events and back again. They comment that while the RHI is not a task, experiencing the RHI involves cognitive flexibility and may thus be associated with the propensity to mind wander and adeptness to switch between tasks. The authors propose four directional hypotheses: those whose minds wander will have a weaker RHI and it will be slower to emerge; conversely, those who are better at task switching will have a stronger RHI and it will be quicker to emerge.

To assess the strength of the RHI, Yeh *et al.* include part of a 9-item questionnaire used by Botvinick and Cohen (1998) to judge the strength of the RHI. They use the first three questions from it, without saying what the first three questions are. This section only makes sense if you have read the Botvinick and Cohen article. These three items are:

It seemed as if I were feeling the touch of the paintbrush in the location where I saw the rubber hand touched.

> It seemed as though the touch I felt was caused by the paintbrush touching the rubber hand.

> I felt as if the rubber hand were my hand. (Botvinick & Cohen, 1998, p. 756)

These questions were answered using 7-point rating scales that ranged from 'strongly agree' (+3) to 'strongly disagree' (−3). Botvinick and Cohen had found that only these three questions produced positive ratings. The remaining questions referred to experiences such as feeling like you owned a third hand, feeling that you had a rubbery hand, or that the rubber hand began to resemble your own hand to the point of skin colour and freckles. Answers to these questions either produced negative ratings or inconsistent ratings, with some people agreeing and some not. Yeh *et al.* therefore selected the three questions that had produced the most consistent positive ratings, which indicated that most of Botvinick and Cohen's participants agreed with them.

Yeh *et al.* include additional questionnaires to assess the possible role of attention in the RHI. The Attentional Control Scale (Derryberry & Reed, 2002) assesses a person's ability to focus attention and to shift attention. The focused attention section includes nine questions such as: 'It's very hard for me to concentrate on a difficult task when there are noises around' (2002, p. 11). The shifting attention section includes 11 questions such as: 'It is difficult for me to co-ordinate my attention between listening and writing required when taking notes during lectures' (2002, p. 11). Participants rated each question on a 4-point scale (1 = 'almost never', 2 = 'sometimes', 3 = 'often', 4 = 'always').

From the attention-focus and attention-shift components of the Attentional Control Scale, Yeh *et al.* produce four more directional hypotheses, although these are only made clear in the Results section. There the hypotheses are clarified as: participants who are better able to focus their attention or shift their attention between tasks will experience a stronger RHI and it will emerge more quickly. Conversely, those less able to focus their attention or shift between tasks will experience a weaker RHI and it will emerge more slowly. There is clearly overlap between these hypotheses and those formulated for the task-switching and mind-wandering tasks.

Methods

Yeh *et al.* recruited 36 participants, some of whom were students and some members of the public. They do not provide the average age, or range of ages, of their participants, or their genders. That impacts the external validity of their study.

They used a standard RHI arrangement: each participant placed both hands on a table, the left hand was occluded from view and a rubber hand placed beside it, in plain view. There were two conditions presented in counterbalanced order. In the synchronous condition, paint brushes were stroked across the five digits on the real, occluded, left hand and rubber hand simultaneously: this should elicit the RHI. In the asynchronous condition, the brush strokes on the real and rubber hands were alternated: this should not elicit a RHI. The brush strokes were applied for 3 minutes. The participants used two foot pedals: the left to signal they were aware the stroking had started and the right to signal they had begun to experience the rubber hand as a part of themselves.

> *Participants were asked to respond, with their right foot, 'as soon as you begin to experience the rubber hand as part of self'. Do you think this instruction would be clear to everyone? Is it a leading question? It clearly tells the participants what the experimenters are expecting should occur.*

Yeh *et al.* claim that asking participants to indicate when the rubber hand is experienced as belonging to the self, with a foot pedal response, is a reliable measure of the strength of the illusion and provides timing data that retrospective reports cannot. They counter the criticism that their participants' responses may have been influenced by an expectation to experience the illusion by saying that some participants did not experience the RHI.

> *Tasks demands are always a problem when people self-report an experience the experimenter clearly expects or hopes will occur. Arguing that asking participants to indicate when the RHI begins is a reliable measure of illusion strength, because some people do not see an illusion, is hardly adequate to counter the criticism that some people will change their behaviour when they know what is expected in an experiment. Some may say they experience it when they do not; others may say they do not experience it when they do. (See Chapter 2 for further discussion of demand characteristics.)*
>
> *Another factor to consider is individual differences. Whenever a subjective measure is taken, such as the time taken to experience the RHI, people differ in how cautious they are before they will acknowledge that they have felt something. Some people are prepared to be cavalier, or are willing to say they felt something if they have just the faintest whiff of an experience, whereas others wait until they are sure they have experienced something before acknowledging it.*

> *This would be a very stressful task for some participants: some people do not even like, for example, counting backwards in sevens from, say, 245. It is a classic way to increase stress and arousal! This task is arguably more difficult. Again, imagine yourself doing this task. How would you feel? Calm? Flustered? Do you think it matters?*

Mind wandering was assessed using a modified version of the Sustained Attention to Response Task, or SART (Robertson *et al.*, 1997). Their participants viewed a stream of letters on a computer screen and had to press the space bar each time one appeared, unless the letter was the target letter 'C'. They chose a target/non-target letter ratio of 1:19 but they do not say how many trials there were, or whether there were practice trials. Yeh *et al.* added 30 'thought probes' during the sequence, which asked each participant whether they were thinking about the task, task performance or matters irrelevant to the task. Mind wandering was assessed by calculating the proportion of times each participant said they were thinking about something other than the task.

Imagine yourself in the experiment. What would you say if you are basically being asked whether you are paying attention or not? Would you admit to daydreaming? Also, by the time you have answered these probe questions twice, you could expect you would be asked them again. Yeh and colleagues do not provide the actual data showing how many times participants admitted to thinking about something other than the task.

In the task-switching experiment, digits appeared above or below the midpoint of a computer screen. When the digit was in the upper portion of the screen, the participant had to decide whether it was odd or even. When it appeared in the lower, they had to decide whether it was greater or less than 5. Reaction times were calculated for trials that followed a switch from the upper to lower location, or vice versa, and compared to the reaction times on repetition trials when the task remained in the same location for the subsequent trial. Task switch trials should yield longer reaction times than repetition trials. Thirty practice trials were followed by 240 experimental trials presented in four blocks. Switch cost was measured as the difference in reaction time between switch and repetition trials. There is no mention of errors; presumably switch cost was calculated from correct responses only. It would, however, have been useful to know the accuracy rate, since this is a difficult task.

Results

In the RHI experiment, Yeh *et al.* report a significant difference between the ratings of illusion strength in the synchronous and asynchronous finger stroking conditions, as expected: their participants experienced the RHI in the synchronous condition mainly (Figure 3.1A).

There is a puzzle when it comes to comparing the RHI onset times in the synchronous and asynchronous conditions. Yeh *et al.* wanted to use the data collected from the asynchronous condition as a baseline, yet in the asynchronous condition people were not expected to experience the RHI, so there would be no onset time to use as a baseline. The authors do not say how they calculated the onset times from those participants who did not experience the RHI in

Figure 3.1 Average RHI questionnaire ratings (A) and 'onset times' (B), presumably in seconds, in the synchronous and asynchronous conditions (error bars represent standard errors of the mean); (C) correlation between RHI strength and 'onset times'. RHI strength is the difference between the RHI ratings in the synchronous and asynchronous conditions; 'onset time' is the difference in onset times in the synchronous and asynchronous conditions. © Yeh *et al.* (2017).

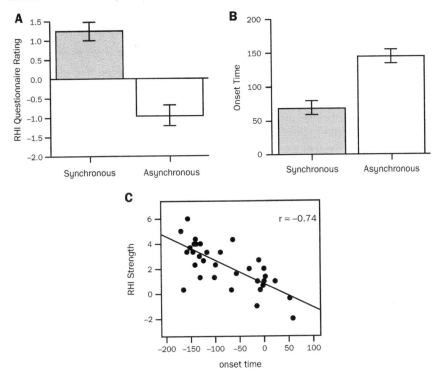

either condition. They nevertheless report that their participants began to experience the illusion more quickly in the synchronous than in the asynchronous condition (Figure 3.1B). They also report a significant negative correlation between the strength of the illusion and onset times (Figure 3.1C). See GQ6 below for further details.

The authors' measures of executive function were their participants' mind-wandering scores, their performance on the task-switching experiment, and their ratings on the two components of the Attention Control Scale (attention-focus and attention-shift). They performed two hierarchical regression analyses using these measures of executive function as predictors, one for the illusion 'onset times' and a second for the illusion strength ratings. In the first regression, they found their participants' attention-shift ratings and their task switch scores contributed to explaining the variance in the illusion 'onset times'. Their mind-wandering scores and attention-focus ratings did not contribute significantly. In the second regression, only the participants' attention-shift ratings contributed to explaining the variance in the illusion strength ratings.

Conclusions

Yeh *et al.* concluded executive functions do play a role in the RHI illusion despite the ridiculousness of adopting a rubber hand as your own: participants who were better at task switching or shifting attention experienced the RHI more strongly and more quickly.

The ten general questions (10GQs)

When this article has been discussed in class, there has been lingering confusion between ordinal and ratio data, the assumptions required to use parametric tests, and what degrees of freedom tell you. In class, each paper is also accompanied by two exercises: questions that direct you to consider particular aspects of each paper (these are presented below, at the end of the discussion of the article). In the past, there has been some difficulty answering these questions in an evaluative and coherent essay, rather than presenting a list of snippets from the text.

1(a). Does the report specify an hypothesis? If so, what is it? Is there more than one? Yeh *et al.* have eight explicit directional hypotheses:

Hypotheses 1 & 2: participants who are better at task switching will experience a stronger RHI: it will be more robust, and it will emerge more quickly.

Hypotheses 3 & 4: participants who have wandering minds will experience a weaker RHI: it will be less robust, and it will emerge more slowly.

Hypotheses 5 & 6: participants who are better able to focus their attention, according to their answers to the Attention Control Scale (ACS), will experience a stronger RHI: it will be more robust, and it will emerge more quickly.

Hypotheses 7 & 8: participants who are better able to shift their attention, according to their answers to the ACS, will experience a stronger RHI: it will be more robust, and it will emerge more quickly.

There is an implied hypothesis that the RHI illusion would be faster to appear and stronger in the synchronous than asynchronous conditions, given the literature cited.

In the Methods section, Yeh et al. define mind-wandering scores as the proportion of 'yes' answers to the probe question that asked whether what their participants were thinking about was irrelevant to the task but, in the Results section, mind wandering is referred to as the SART score. Only the probe question directly assesses mind wandering and so is, presumably, the measure that was used.

1(b). What background or rationale is provided as justification for any hypothesis? Yeh *et al.* wished to examine the role of higher cognitive, or executive, functions in the RHI and focus principally on attention. As described in the synopsis, the background provided is somewhat patchy. While they provide a clear account of the illusion itself, they misquote some of the relevant research and omit other relevant work. For example, they cite Armel and Ramachandran (2003) in support of the assertion that the fake object, or the to-be-embodied object, must look like a plausible body part, a hand, whereas Armel and Ramachandran reported that their participants had embodied part of a table. They maintain that the rubber hand must be close to the real hand, whereas Armel and Ramachandran reported the RHI persisted even when the rubber hand was 3 feet away from the participant.

When justifying their decision to explore the role of executive functions in multisensory integration and the RHI, Yeh *et al.* first cite studies on the role of attention on the integration of vision and hearing, not multisensory integration relevant to the RHI or the sense of the body. They cite just one study on the role of attention in the integration of vision and touch. They comment there has been less research on interactions between attention, touch and vision than between attention, hearing and vision. It may be true that there has been less, but it is disingenuous to imply there has been very little. In September 2020, a citation search using the words 'rubber hand illusion' and 'attention' yielded 3,700 articles; swapping 'attention' for (i) 'executive function' produced 231, (ii) 'mind wandering' produced 106, and (iii) 'task switching' produced 95. Most of these citations were published before 2017 when Yeh *et al.* submitted their article. Instead of claiming there had been little work done in this area, Yeh and colleagues could have emphasised a relatively new aspect of their study: measuring the onset time of the illusion rather than relying only on retrospective subjective self-reports. Measuring the onset time of the RHI has been highlighted in a recent review of their article (Kalckert, 2018).

Yeh *et al.* also assume the reader knows some of the research they are referring to: their discussion of the questionnaire used by Botvinick and Cohen (1998) to measure the strength of the RHI, for example, makes no sense unless you have read that article, as they do not include the three questions that they chose to use (the three questions used from Botvinick and Cohen's questionnaire are included in the synopsis). They discuss proprioceptive drift in relation to the RHI, without explaining what it is. It becomes clear if you read the article by Botvinick and Cohen, but without that missing detail this section is unintelligible.

2(a). Specify all the variables in the investigation and indicate what sort of variables they are (e.g. dependent vs. independent, manipulated, controlled, nuisance, confounding). Specify what level of measurement has been achieved for each dependent variable (nominal, ordinal, interval, ratio). For the RHI, there was one independent variable: synchrony (whether the hidden and rubber hands were stroked with a paintbrush synchronously or asynchronously).

There were two dependent variables for the RHI: time of illusion onset (ratio) and the ratings from the Botvinick and Cohen (1998) scale that assesses the strength of the RHI. The participants rated three questions on a scale from –3 to +3, denoting 'strongly disagree' to 'strongly agree'. This type of scale is typically considered to yield interval data (see Chapter 2). An average (mean) score was calculated for each participant in each condition.

Additional dependent variables were as follows: (1) mind-wandering scores – the proportion of times the participant acknowledged thinking about matters irrelevant to the task, which was asked 30 times during a Sustained Attention to Response Task, SART (ratio); (2) task-switching scores – the difference in reaction times between consecutive switch and repetition trials (ratio); (3) the average attention-switch scores from the ACS (it consists of 4-point scales to indicate the level of agreement with each question, where 1 = 'almost never', 2 = 'sometimes', 3 = 'often' and 4 = 'always' – these scales are ordinal yet the data are treated as interval); and (4) the average attention-focus scores from the ACS (ordinal, also treated as interval). An average was calculated for the attention-switch and attention-focus ACS questions.

They have a confound in the task-switching experiment, since they have introduced the Simon effect (see GQ3 below). Nuisance variables include participant bias (willingness to comply), experimenter bias (prompting) and possibly participant embarrassment but there is no reason to think that they varied systematically across conditions, so they are not confounding variables.

2(b). Do the selected variables address the research hypothesis/ hypotheses? Yeh *et al.* wanted to study associations between attention and attentional control and the strength and onset time of the RHI (this is the concept they wished to explore). They chose tasks that addressed issues in attention such as focus, control and flexibility (these are how they chose to operationalise the concept they wanted to study). The RHI illusion was induced with a standard procedure and there is a close correspondence between the research hypotheses and some of the dependent variables. For example, task switching and the ACS are standard tests of a person's ability to allocate or focus attention appropriately for the task at hand.

On the other hand, the assessment of mind wandering and the RHI rating scales are not standard, so more detail would have been useful. In particular, consistency when describing what was used to assess mind wandering would have helped to clarify what the mind-wandering variable was ('yes' responses to the thought probe questions, or the SART score, presumably the former). It would also have been helpful to include the content of the three RHI rating scales from Botvinick and Cohen (1998). If both of these dependent variables had been presented accurately, it would have clarified their appropriateness to test the hypotheses on mind wandering and the strength of the RHI.

3. What did the participants have to do? (briefly) Is the study easily replicable? There were four sections to the study: (1) the standard RHI arrangement and procedure; (2) a SART, combined with 30 questions that asked what the participant was thinking about; (3) a task-switching experiment; and (4) the ACS. The RHI, SART and task-switching experiment were presented in a counterbalanced order, while the ACS was always completed at the end.

Several comments can be made about their task-switching experiment. Participants were asked to judge whether a number presented on a computer screen was greater or less than 5 (if on the lower part of the screen) or whether it was odd or even (if on the upper part). The numbers could appear at one of four locations: upper left, upper right, lower left, lower right. Using their left and right hands, their participants pressed the letter 'A' if the number displayed was odd and in the upper part of the screen, or if the digit was greater than 5 and in the lower part of the screen (left hand). They pressed the ';' key for the other trials (right hand) (see Figure 3.2).

Figure 3.2 The task-switch procedure used by Yeh et al. Digits (1–4, 6–9) were presented at one of four locations around a central fixation cross. Participants had to press 'A' on a standard keyboard when digits were odd and in the upper part of the computer screen, or when digits were greater than 5 and in the lower part; or they pressed ';' when digits were even and in the upper part of the screen, or less than 5 and in the lower part. Consecutive trials that required the same type of response (e.g. deciding when digits presented in the upper part of the screen were odd on sequential trials) count as task-repetition trials. Consecutive trials that required different types of response (e.g. on the first trial, deciding whether a digit presented in the lower part of the screen was greater than 5; then, on the subsequent trial, deciding whether the digit was odd when presented in the upper part of the screen) count as task-switch trials. © Yeh et al. (2017).

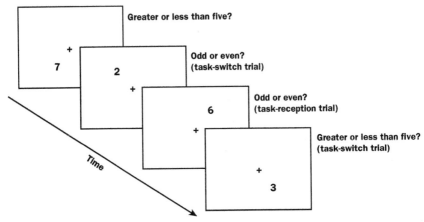

Having four locations is a good way to force participants to do the task as intended: had they only had a single upper and lower location, participants could adopt a different strategy to the one intended to make the task easier. For example, if they only had to attend to one location, say, upper, they could just look for odd numbers or numbers greater than 5 and press 'A'; otherwise they would press ';'. Some people do try to make the tasks easier if they can!

Unfortunately, they introduced a confound, the Simon effect (Simon & Rudell, 1967; Simon, 1969), with their choice of keys (Figure 3.3). The numbers, whether above or below the midline, were also either left or right of fixation. This meant there would be a tendency to press the key on the right (or left) when the digit appeared on the right (or left) regardless of whether the digit was odd or even, or greater or less than 5. To be accurate, participants must suppress the tendency to push the key corresponding to the stimulus location, and that lengthens reaction time. Or they can press immediately according to the stimulus location and make more errors.

For the SART, Yeh *et al.* do not specify how many trials there were, or whether there was any practice. Apart from that, the study is mostly replicable, although anyone wishing to do so would want to change the response keys for the task-switching experiment to avoid the Simon effect. With both an up-down and left-right component to the task, however, it is hard to imagine what an appropriate pair of key responses could be.

4(a). What experimental design was used? This is a within-group or repeated-measures design, as each participant completed every section of the study.

Figure 3.3 Illustration of the Simon effect that confounds the task switching task used by Yeh *et al.* Participants made their responses using their left (when pressing 'A') and right (when pressing ';') hands. The four digits in each panel are shown to illustrate odd and even digits, greater and less than 5, for each location: during the experiment, only one digit was presented at one of the four locations on each trial (see Figure 3.2). The 'A' and ';' symbols show the correct response for each digit location. The unenclosed digits show trials where the location of the key on the keyboard corresponds to the location of the digit on screen: response times should be fastest for these trials. The enclosed digits show trials where the location of the key on the keyboard and the location of the digit on screen are inconsistent and, to be accurate, participants must suppress a tendency to respond with the hand that coincides with the location of the digit on screen.

 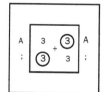 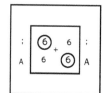 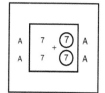

4(b). Do the method and design address the research hypothesis/ hypotheses? The repeated-measures, or within-subjects, design is essential in any study of associations between cognitive processes and the experience of an illusion due to individual differences in the experience of the illusion, or in the criterion each participant used to report that they do. Yeh et al. point out that the experience of the RHI can vary widely between participants, and some do not experience it at all. There are also individual differences in people's ability to focus their attention or tendency to drift off into daydreaming. The assessments of the illusion and performance on the attention tasks had to be performed by every participant to minimise the effects of these individual differences.

Yeh et al. counterbalanced the assessments of the RHI, mind wandering and task-switching ability, but the ACS was always presented at the end. Counterbalancing is essential in repeated-measures designs so that factors such as boredom or tiredness, which are always present, do not systematically affect responses on each task. Yeh et al. do not think that presenting the ACS scale at the end would have biased responses on the ACS since it measures attentional control in general. The authors do not say how long their test session lasted, but tiredness or boredom could affect the participants' motivation or diligence when finally rating the ACS questions. The participants had also just completed attentionally demanding tasks in what must have been a tiring session. If they felt they had performed poorly at some stage, that could have affected their responses when they came to rate themselves on the ACS. The ACS could have been administered in a separate session so that their responses would not be affected by their perceived performance on the other tasks.

It is usual to include synchronous and asynchronous stroking of the hands when assessing the RHI, as the asynchronous condition provides a control to check that people are responding truthfully: the RHI should not be experienced in the asynchronous condition or, if it is, it should be weak. Although the RHI illusion was induced with a standard procedure, participants made their responses with both feet, which is unusual, and Yeh et al. do not provide references to other work that has shown foot responses can be a reliable indicator of timing.

The other tasks and questionnaires are more problematic, leading to some reservations: they are unclear, vague or leading. For example, Yeh et al. report that task switching was the difference in reaction times between task switching on consecutive trials, and task repetition on consecutive trials. They do not, however, report accuracy and whether their calculations were only for those trials where their participants' response was correct. If all trials are included, whether correct or incorrect, the validity of their task switch measure is undermined. Presumably they included only correct task-switch and task-repetition trials, but then the average data for different observers will be based on a different number of trials depending on how well each person performed this (difficult) task. An average based on 15 correct trials may be less reliable than one based on 50.

The questions used to assess mind wandering addressed whether the participant was thinking about the task, about task performance or about matters irrelevant to the task. It is not clear why they needed the first two questions, or whether the participants would know how to differentiate them, and answers to these questions were discarded anyway. The three questions are also leading and they raise the question whether their participants would admit to daydreaming in an experiment. Additionally, by the time the participants had answered these probe questions a couple of times, they would likely know that they were going to be asked again, which could affect their subsequent responses. There is, therefore, a possibility of floor effects, if participants selected one of the task-oriented questions as the trials progressed. As we are not given the data for this task, it is impossible to tell.

5. What comparisons were chosen for statistical analysis? Yeh *et al.* compared the onset time and the strength of the RHI in the synchronous and asynchronous conditions. They also looked at the relationship between onset times and illusion strength. Finally, they looked at how both the onset time and the strength of RHI were influenced by their participants' ability to task switch, their susceptibility for their thoughts to wander, and their level of attentional control.

6. What analysis was used? Was it appropriate? The data are the time taken to experience the illusion (ratio); the average illusion strength ratings from three questions (interval); the proportion of trials when their participants confessed to daydreaming (from 30 mind wandering questions, ratio); the average number of statements endorsed from the attention-shift and attention-focus subscales of the ACS (11 questions and 9 questions, respectively, ordinal but treated as interval). The level or measurement is appropriate for parametric testing except for the ACS ratings. Tests for normality or homogeneity of variance are not reported.

The data that are presented for the RHI are in graphical form only but, from these, numerical values for the average scores and standard errors can be estimated. For the RHI intensity rating (Figure 3.1A), their participants agreed with the statements about embodying the rubber hand in the synchronous condition (mean rating ± 1 standard error (SE): 1.24 ± 0.2) but disagreed with those statements in the asynchronous condition (mean rating ± 1 SE: –0.95 ± 0.3). Recall that the scales ranged from +3 ('strongly agree') to –3 ('strongly disagree'). Here, the standard errors are similar in size for the synchronous and asynchronous conditions, which indicates comparable variances in the two conditions. Their size relative to the mean rating in each condition gives an indication of how well the mean summarises the underlying data: in Figure 3.1A, the standard errors are relatively small compared to the size of the mean rating scores in each condition, which indicates the means in each condition provide a reasonable summary of the underlying data, that is, the data are not widely dispersed around the mean values.

As mentioned in the synopsis, Yeh *et al.* do not say what they did with those participants who did not experience the RHI in either condition. The authors nevertheless report that their participants began to experience the illusion more quickly in the synchronous (average onset time ± 1 SE: 70 ± 10 seconds) than in the asynchronous condition (145 ± 10 seconds; Figure 3.1B). The standard errors are relatively small compared to the size of the mean 'onset times', indicating again that the averages in each condition provide a reasonable summary of the underlying data.

The RHI questionnaire ratings and 'onset times' in the synchronous and asynchronous conditions were compared with two related *t*-tests. Since the data are ratio and the standard errors are comparable across the two conditions for both RHI ratings and onset times, related *t*-tests are appropriate. These *t*-tests do not link directly to one of their hypotheses but, if you are assessing the RHI (or any illusion) with two conditions and in only one condition should the illusion be experienced, you need to demonstrate that the illusion was indeed experienced (even if not by everyone/not on every trial). The two *t*-tests show that they did get the RHI for both illusion strength ratings and what they call onset times.

One issue is to work out what the onset time data are for those who did not experience the RHI. The *t*-test had 35 degrees of freedom, and there were 36 participants, so all participants were included in the analysis. Yeh *et al.* decided to give each participant who did not experience the RHI an 'onset time' of 180 seconds, the duration that their hands were being stroked on each trial. The data presented for the 'onset times' in the asynchronous condition are thereby, at best, misleading, as they include data that are not onset times. The average 'onset time' in the asynchronous condition is 145 seconds, not 180 seconds, which indicates a few participants did experience the RHI in the asynchronous condition (or indicated that they did), which brings the onset time down from 180 to 145 seconds. What is plotted in Figure 3.1B is, therefore, a mixture of entries capped at 180, together with actual onset times for the few who did experience the illusion in the asynchronous condition. It is arguably inappropriate to perform a *t*-test between real onset times from the synchronous condition, and capped 'onset times' from the asynchronous condition.

Yeh *et al.* also report a significant negative correlation between the strength of the illusion and 'onset times' ($r = -0.74$, presumably Pearson's correlation coefficient). In Figure 3.1C, the data points cluster fairly well around the line of best fit, and there do not appear to be outliers. As for the *t*-tests, the data fit the assumptions for a parametric test. This correlation is again not directly linked to an hypothesis, but if you have two dependent variables showing different aspects of the same illusion, it would be usual to check to see whether the two correlated: did those who rated the RHI as more vivid in the synchronous than in the asynchronous condition also experience it more quickly? The answer appears to be 'yes', with the caveat that their measure of 'onset time' is not actually onset time.

To assess the associations between the various measures of attention and the RHI, Yeh *et al.* conducted two hierarchical regression analyses, one using the illusion strength ratings as the dependent variable, and one using 'onset times'. Both dependent variables were the difference scores between the synchronous and asynchronous conditions (i.e. the data presented in Figure 3.1C). For each, the predictor variables were entered in the following order: 1 – mind wandering (now referred to as the SART score rather than the proportion of times the participant admitted to daydreaming); 2 – the average attention-shift rating from the ACS; 3 – the switch cost from the task-switching experiment; 4 – the average attention-focus rating from the ACS. They claim this order had been mentioned in the Introduction, yet there is no such explicit mention.

The authors may be referring to their list of hypotheses presented in the Introduction, which are in this order:

1 The role of executive functions is to refocus participants' attention to external task-related stimuli, leading to a stronger RHI.
2 Mind wanderers will be less susceptible to the RHI.
3 Better task switchers will have an enhanced RHI and will experience the RHI earlier.
4 People who have better attention control, assessed with the two components of the ACS, will have stronger RHI experiences and will experience the RHI earlier. The authors do not differentiate between attention-focus and attention-shift from the ACS.

This order does not, however, map onto the order of variables entered into their regression models. While mind wandering was mentioned first and perhaps was the reason it entered the regression model first, their list does not explain why attention-shift came before attention-focus, or why task-switching was positioned in-between them.

7. What was the main result? In the RHI experiment, Yeh *et al.* reported a significant difference between the ratings of illusion strength in the synchronous and asynchronous conditions (paired sample *t*-test, Figure 3.1A). The difference was in the predicted direction: on average, their participants agreed with the statements about embodying the rubber hand in the synchronous condition, but disagreed with those statements in the asynchronous condition.

The authors also reported a significant difference in RHI 'onset time' between the synchronous and asynchronous conditions (paired sample *t*-test, Figure 3.1B). The difference was again in the predicted direction: on average, their participants began to experience the illusion more quickly in the synchronous than in the asynchronous condition.

Yeh *et al.* reported a significant negative correlation between the strength of the RHI (assessed by subtracting the asynchronous ratings from the synchronous ones) and 'onset time' (similarly, the difference between the synchronous and asynchronous 'onset times', $r = -0.74$, Figure 3.1C). Those who reported the greatest difference in ownership of the rubber hand in the synchronous and asynchronous conditions had the most negative 'onset times' (negative as these are difference scores), that is, they experienced the RHI more quickly than participants whose difference in ratings of the RHI in each condition was less marked.

For the hierarchical regression analyses, Yeh *et al.* report R^2, ΔR^2, F and F of increased R^2. They do not present any data for mind wandering but, whatever the distribution of these data, they did not contribute significantly to either of their hierarchical regression analyses (both $F < 1$) and mind wandering could have been removed. Mind wandering is also ignored in their interpretation of the results from their regression models.

The regression using RHI 'onset time' showed that the model with the first three predictors explained the variance in the data as well as model 4, that is, model 4 did not add any predictive weight (mind wandering was retained in the model despite contributing nothing). Attention-shift ratings were negatively related to the onset time ($r = -0.41$), and switch costs were positively related ($r = 0.39$): those who reported being able to switch their attention from one task to another, and those who had small switch costs when forced to switch from one task to another, responded more quickly when they experienced the RHI in the synchronous condition (Figure 3.4).

Figure 3.4 Correlations between the RHI 'onset time' and (A) attention-shift ratings from the ACS and (B) switch costs from the task-switching test. © Yeh *et al.* (2017).

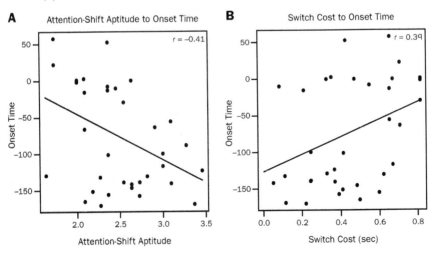

Figure 3.5 Correlations between the rating of RHI strength and attention-shift ratings from the ACS. © Yeh *et al.* (2017).

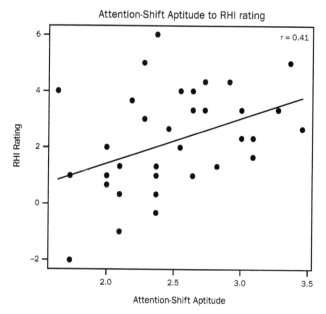

For the regression using the strength of the RHI from the Botvinick and Cohen questionnaire ratings, the model with only two predictors explained the data as well as models with three or four predictors (mind wandering was again retained in the model but again ignored as it contributed nothing). Attention-shift ratings were positively related to the RHI strength ($r = 0.41$): those with higher attention-shift ratings had a stronger experience of the RHI (Figure 3.5).

8. What conclusions were drawn? Were they valid? Generally, Yeh *et al.* concluded that executive functions do play a role in the RHI illusion despite the absurdity of adopting a rubber hand as your own. Multisensory or low-level sensory processing explanations for the RHI alone are not sufficient. Models that include cognitive flexibility can also explain individual differences in the experience of the RHI, which is a reasonable suggestion. More specifically, the authors' main conclusions from the data are that:

1 The ability to switch between tasks plays a modulatory role on the 'onset time' of the RHI, whether that ability is assessed by task-switching or by self-report using the attention-switch component of the ACS. This is valid from the data collected and the analyses

performed, with the caveat that 'onset time' is not a true reflection of onset times, as those who did not experience the RHI were given an onset time of 180 seconds, so taking the difference in onset time between the conditions misrepresents the concept of onset time.

2   The self-report ratings from the attention-focus questions of the ACS were also correlated with the ratings of the strength of the RHI. This conclusion is valid.

3   The authors speculate that task switching and attention shifting may be trainable, which could enhance a person's experience of the RHI, but there is no evidence for this in their study.

4   They consider that completing the ACS last would not bias responses, as the questions it asks are not directly related to the specific content of the other tasks (mind wandering, task switching and the RHI). The content of the questions and their relevance to the specific details of each task, however, do negate order effects is a rather weak assertion, as order effects include boredom and tiredness. They do not mention how long their test session lasted for.

9. What are your main criticisms of the report?

1   Allocating an onset time of 180 seconds when people did not experience the RHI, which tarnishes their comparisons of the synchronous and asynchronous onset times. What should have been reported is the onset time for those few who did experience the illusion in the asynchronous condition and how many of them there were. Equally, the number who did not see the illusion in the synchronous condition should have been reported, particularly given the authors' reliance on some people not experiencing the illusion in the synchronous condition as an argument for the relevance of cognitive factors influencing the RHI. The eligible number of participants for the correlation between onset time and RHI strength would plummet, but it would allow a direct assessment of the correlation between RHI strength and actual onset times in the two conditions.

2   The Simon effect confounds the reaction time data for the task-switching experiment.

3   Yeh et al. provide no clear justification for the order they entered the variables in their hierarchical regression analyses.

4   In the RHI experiment, participants would know that the experimenter hopes that they will experience the illusion. This is likely to affect some responses, as some people are more ready to comply and others are more willing to resist (see Chapter 2 for further discussion of demand characteristics).

5   Yeh et al. do not provide details of their sample: average age, age range, even their gender.

6 Some of the data were collected but not presented. Without these data, the reader cannot know if the data collected are sensible. When standard tests are used, it is useful to have the data presented so they can be compared to other studies that have used similar measures, to check that the data collected are comparable to those reported previously. For example, Yeh *et al.* present data for their attention-shift ratings in their figures 3 and 4, but the attention-focus ratings are not presented. Other data that were not presented:

- The results of the SART. It would have been useful to know how many incorrect or correct responses there were for each participant and, when the 30 thought probe questions were interspersed, how many followed a correct response? A tally of correct/incorrect responses and their proximity to the thought probe questions would have given additional information about how well the participants were attending to the SART.

- The data from the mind-wandering questions. Since the questions were presented 30 times, the participants may expect to be asked the questions on further trials having been asked them for the second time, and that may change their responses on the SART and on truthfulness: as mentioned, would you agree you were daydreaming when asked? There may, therefore, have been floor effects.

- Accuracy data for the task-switching task. Presumably there is a difference in accuracy for the two types of task (consecutive switch trials or consecutive repetition trials), but this is not mentioned. Neither is it mentioned whether the switch costs were calculated for correct responses only.

7 Finally, some of the exposition is overly verbose, and sometimes previous work is referred to in insufficient detail. The lack of detail has already been mentioned for the Botvinick and Cohen questionnaire and the reference to proprioceptive drift without explanation (see the synopsis). Additional examples include mention of the role of interoceptive, exteroceptive signals, the cardiovascular system and histamine. The inclusion of these examples makes little sense without reading the original articles. Instruction of what the scientific method should hope to explain, and disparaging comments on the motivation of other researchers, are unnecessary.

10. What are the main strengths of the report? Yeh *et al.* present an interesting addition to traditional studies of the RHI by including illusion onset time as well as subjective ratings of the illusion strength, although that brought with it difficulties to define an onset time when the illusion was not experienced. They were not the first to introduce onset time, but it is a relatively recent addition.

Their focus on associations between the experience of the RHI and cognitive flexibility is also an addition to traditional studies of the RHI, although their endeavour is undermined by some lapses in experimental procedure and in the presentation of their data. The arguments to include each test is, nevertheless, clear and well-motivated.

Exercises

1 Do the authors provide adequate details of prior research on the rubber hand illusion? Extract the main explanatory models. Is the inclusion of attention tasks well justified? Evaluate the specific predictions the authors make and comment on how well the methods chosen can test them.

2 Which statistical analyses were performed? Were they all appropriate? Were they all justified, given the authors' hypotheses? Were they all clearly presented? Comment on the pattern of results and evaluate the authors' conclusions. Comment specifically on the authors' discussion of mind wandering, task switching and attention shifting, in light of the regression analyses. Is their discussion complete?

Blaesi, S., & Wilson, M. (2010). The mirror reflects both ways: Action influences perception of others. *Brain and Cognition, 72*(2), 306–309. https://doi.org/10.1016/j.bandc.2009.10.001.

You will likely have had the experience of walking down a street when another person approaches and, as you try to move to pass them, find the pair of you mirroring each other's actions: you step to one side to avoid colliding with them and they step in the same direction, you try to step to the other side and they follow suit and this imitation, sometimes referred to as a dance, continues for as long as you look at each other. If, on the other hand, you see a person walking down the street on a possible collision trajectory and one of you stares at the ground instead of looking at the potential collider, you can pass without either the side-to-side shuffle or a collision. This is an illustration of the mirror-neuron system in action (for an early review, see Rizzolatti & Craighero, 2004). Another everyday example is when chatting with a friend: should they touch their face during the conversation, you may find yourself touching yours as if mirroring their action. The mirror-neuron system involves a complex network of visual and motor areas that spans occipital, temporal, parietal and frontal regions. It is activated when a person observes another person performing an action: you tend do the same action.

In an interesting twist on this effect, Blaesi and Wilson (2010) turned the question around and asked whether a person performing an action influences their perception of another person performing a similar action. They were not the first to ask this question, but their novel contribution is their discussion of who to test and what sort of actions to choose. Their article raises important issues concerning internal and external validity of an experiment.

Synopsis

Introduction

Blaesi and Wilson (2010) comment on the paucity of studies that have addressed whether concurrent action influences perception. They provide a brief introduction to previous research in the areas of sport and dance and point out that expertise in performing an action can be confounded with expertise in observing the same actions. For example, if athletes or dancers are recruited for an experiment, and they are asked to watch a sporting event or a dance routine, the participants will have expertise in both performing and observing their chosen sport or dance, so the two cannot be disentangled. If commentators are recruited as a comparison group, even if they are ex-players or dancers themselves, they are likely to have more recent experience observing actions than executing them. Equally, many fans perform or have performed the same sports or dances, if not at a professional level, and they too will have more experience observing than performing the actions. Blaesi and Wilson conclude that if commentators or fans are compared to expert athletes or dancers on some measure of accuracy of the movements, expertise in performance and in observation are confounded as they differ between the groups.

> *Recap: Confounds* are unwanted variables that vary **systematically** across different experimental conditions (e.g. tiredness, boredom) or between different groups of participants in an experiment (e.g. expert, non-expert). They compromise the internal validity of an experiment. Participant selection also affects an experiment's external validity.

The authors cite two fMRI studies that tested experienced dancers (ballet dancers and capoeiristas) and participants with experience in neither. They reported distinct patterns of activity in brain regions that underlie motor activity when the experts observed dance sequences that they themselves could perform, compared to when they observed unfamiliar dance sequences (Calvo-Merino *et al.*, 2005, 2006). This is consistent with action influencing perception, at least in those expert in particular actions. There were no differences in brain activity when non-experts viewed either ballet or capoeira.

Blaesi and Wilson then cite studies that have combined activities familiar to most people, such as walking or cycling, with an additional component. For example, Casile and Giese (2006) trained blindfolded participants on a novel motor task: walking with atypical swinging arm movements. The authors then asked them to judge point-light walkers with normal or atypical arm movements. (Point-light walkers are animated cartoons of walking 'figures' where the head, torso and limbs are represented by little dots; there is no other information that a person might be seen. When the dots are stationary, they just look like a collection of dots but, once the dots move in a way analogous to a person walking, they can give a compelling impression of a walking figure, referred to as perceiving biological motion.) People trained in the novel walking pattern were indeed slightly better at recognising a point-light figure performing the atypical arm action they had been trained to perform, when interspersed in a sequence of other atypical arm actions.

Blaesi and Wilson comment that most of these studies confound actions and rhythms, so any effects on subsequent perception cannot be unambiguously attributed to performing the action rather than to recognising the rhythm. That is, any effects of neural *motor* systems on perception are inferred rather than demonstrated. Here they wish to test for a dynamic relationship between action and perception. They then briefly cite several studies in which participants had to hold a particular posture for long periods of time. They point out that feedback from a maintained posture habituates, or declines, rapidly, making any possible effect of maintaining a posture over time, while judging the posture of others, ineffective. They present this background to justify their choice of actions: smiling and opening a pair of scissors. These actions avoid the confound of rhythm and are repeated throughout the experimental session so that the postures are not maintained for long periods of time.

The authors did not, however, ask their participants to smile: if a person is asked to smile multiple times while viewing an image of someone smiling or frowning, it would not be difficult to work out what the study was about. To avoid these 'demand characteristics', their participants were asked instead to hold a pen between their teeth. This action supposedly engages the same muscles as those used when smiling, but people are apparently unaware that it is a manipulation to mimic a smile. Three studies are cited that have used this technique as such a surrogate. Blaesi and Wilson suggest it is, therefore, a way to demonstrate an effect of muscle engagement on perception.

Recap: Demand characteristics. If participants can work out what the study is about, that can affect how they respond. See Chapter 2 for further details.

Blaesi and Wilson do not cite prior research that used such a surrogate for the scissor-opening action in their second experiment; the scissors task appears to be novel. Their justification is that the emotional state of each participant may be affected by performing the 'smiling' pen action. Similarly, the emotional state each participant brings to the experiment may affect their performance. The second experiment with scissors was, therefore, conducted to eliminate any effect that the participants' emotional state may have on their performance. You could wonder why they used smiling and frowning faces in the first place.

Methods

For the first experiment, 11 images were constructed of the same face, which showed a woman smiling at one end of the series and frowning at the other end. They created intermediate images between the smile and the frown by morphing the images to construct a scale with a neutral facial expression somewhere near the middle of the series of images (Figure 3.6).

For the second experiment, 11 computer-generated images of a hand were generated, which showed a continuum from having the thumb and the first two fingers extended and the fourth and fifth fingers curled, to having all five digits extended (Figure 3.7). The images displayed right hands with the thumb touching the chin of a schematic face, the fingers oriented perpendicular to the face. This is a rather artificial posture, and the authors provide no reason for selecting it. Intermediate images for each series, face or hand, were digitally morphed in 10% increments. References are provided for the morphing procedure.

Figure 3.6 The range of affective face stimuli (happy/sad) used in Experiment 1. Image 1, as used by Blaesi and Wilson, depicted the sad face, image 11 depicted the happy face. These images originally came from a study on American sign language. Blaesi and Wilson removed the hands so that only the faces were presented. Reprinted from *Cognition*, 110(2), McCullough S, Emmorey K. Categorical perception of affective and linguistic facial expressions, 208-212, Copyright 2009 with permission from Elsevier.

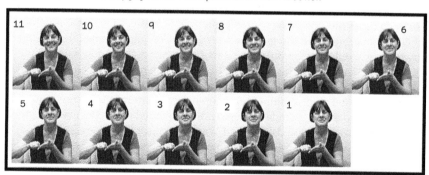

Figure 3.7 The range of hand stimuli (all four fingers extended/two fingers curled) used in Experiment 2. Image 1 shows all digits extended and image 11 shows two fingers curled. These images also originally came from a study on American sign language. © Emmorey, McCullough and Brentari (2003).

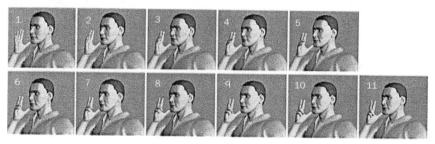

In Experiment 1, there were two conditions, which were alternated on consecutive trials: participants either held a pen between their teeth, pointing away from their nose, or they did not.[2] They were instructed not to let their lips touch the pen. As the pen/no-pen conditions were alternated, the faces on screen were presented in a pseudorandom order. Each of the 11 faces was presented 15 times, making a total of 165 trials for each condition and 330 trials in total, presented in 15 blocks of 22 trials. The task was to judge whether the image on screen was happy or sad (Blaesi and Wilson use the words 'frown' and 'sad' interchangeably).

In Experiment 2, there were again two conditions: participants either held small scissors that only allowed the use of the thumb and the first two fingers, or they held large scissors that required the use of the thumb and all four fingers. This time, the conditions were blocked and the participants had to open the scissors at the start of each trial, when the image appeared on screen, and close them when the image was removed. The task was to decide whether the image on screen displayed three or five digits extended.

> These are peculiar tasks, and that has implications for both internal and external validity. It is always a good idea to imagine yourself being a participant in an experiment. First, consider placing a pen in and out of your mouth on 330 consecutive trials while looking at a face on a screen: what would you be thinking while being asked to do this? Would you feel self-conscious? Second, consider opening and closing either a large or a small pair of scissors multiple times while looking at a schematic face and a hand: boredom, bewilderment and muscle fatigue may have crept in. If an effect was found in either experiment, what could that tell you? Could the results be generalised to other situations?

Participants in both experiments were students who participated for course credit: 28 in Experiment 1 (although three were excluded for guessing the point of the study) and 22 in Experiment 2 (one was excluded for not following the instructions). In both experiments, the ruse was telling the participants that they were being tested on their ability to multitask.

Results

In their first experiment, Blaesi and Wilson calculated, for each person, the image on the range from 'sad' (given scale point 1) to 'happy' (given scale point 11) that yielded 50% of judgements being classified as happy (which is equivalent to the image that produced 50% of responses being classified as sad). This 50% point they termed the threshold for perceiving happy faces (Blaesi and Wilson use the words 'happy' and 'smile', and 'frown' and 'sad' interchangeably). The authors reported a significant group difference between the 'pen in teeth' and 'no pen in teeth' conditions (paired sample t-test). The difference was in the predicted direction: when participants were 'smiling' (holding a pen between their teeth), the threshold was slightly lower on the scale (i.e. a more frowning face) than when they did not. That is, when their participants held the pen between their teeth, they judged more of the images as smiling than when they did not. The mean difference between the thresholds in the 'pen in teeth' and 'no pen in teeth' conditions was rather small, however, despite being statistically significant (scale points 5.22 and 5.33, respectively, one-tenth of a scale point; Figure 3.8A). Blaesi and Wilson only provide a graph of the data for one participant (Figure 3.8B), which shows a difference of just over one scale point – but this person's data are not representative of the average data (Figure 3.8A).

Figure 3.8 (A) The mean percentage 'smile' responses for each of the 11 images in the 'pen in teeth' and 'no pen in teeth' trials. This graph was generated using the means, standard errors, t-test value (2.35) and significance level ($p = 0.028$) reported by Blaesi and Wilson. The one graph that is presented by Blaesi and Wilson shows the data for one participant. This is illustrated in (B) (this is a cartoon for illustration purposes using fictional – not the actual – data, but the shape of the curves in B are similar to their published figure). This participant is clearly not well represented by the group averages (depicted in A).

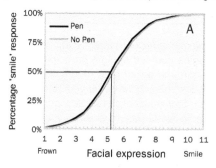 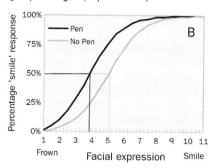

For Experiment 2, Blaesi and Wilson defined the threshold that produced 50% of responses as the image that displayed the thumb and two fingers extended, and the ring and little finger curled (which is equivalent to the image that produced 50% of responses when all five digits were extended). They did not provide a graph of the data. They reported a significant group difference between the large and small scissor conditions (a second paired sample t-test). The difference was apparently in the predicted direction: when participants were using the large scissors, the 50% threshold was slightly larger (mean of 3.73) than when using the small scissors (mean of 3.38). They conclude that, when using the small scissors, their participants judged more of the images as displaying two curled fingers than when using the large scissors.

The missing part of the authors' argument is that, when people use the small scissors, the thumb, index and middle fingers, which are used to open and close the scissors, are fairly straight when they are inserted into the scissors' handles, and the ring and little finger are curled, tucked into the palm of their hand. Equally, when using the large scissors, for their argument to work, the thumb and all four fingers must be assumed to be fairly straight when inserted into the scissors' handles. It is quite possible, however, to have all fingers and the thumb curled, akin to a fist, when using large scissors (it is instructive to try this for yourself and look at the posture of your fingers: the thumb is most likely to be straight whatever the size of the scissors, but the fingers can be equally curled for both scissor sizes).

Conclusions

Blaesi and Wilson conclude that they have shown the mirror system can indeed yield bi-directional effects on perception: what we see can affect our actions and our actions can affect what we see. They comment this is plausible, as neural connections between two areas of the brain are likely to be reciprocal and that has advantages. For example, imitating the actions of another person aids social and emotional understanding and empathy. Equally, they suggest top-down influences from motor to occipital areas could aid perception by making it faster and more accurate, which would be useful in changing environments.

There is no direct evidence that the mirror system underlies these results. Their appeals to social understanding, empathy, or faster and more accurate perception are entirely speculative.

The ten general questions (10GQs)

When this was discussed in class, students struggled to identify the hypotheses when they were not explicitly stated. Extracting the hypotheses is pivotal to understanding a paper. There is always at least one. You cannot move on without finding the hypotheses, since the various parts of your assessment of an article (the choice of variables, the experimental design, the statistical analyses, the conclusions drawn) require you to relate each back to the hypotheses. Some students also struggled to decide on the level of measurement of the dependent variables because a single value (50% happy or 50% digits extended) was extracted from both set of images for each participant using probit analyses.

1(a). Does the report specify an hypothesis? If so, what is it? Is there more than one? Blaesi and Wilson have two directional hypotheses, one for each experiment, although they are not explicitly stated. In Experiment 1, the stimuli are 11 images of a face whose expression lies on a continuum from 'frown' to 'smile' (Figure 3.6). They expected that participants would judge more of the face stimuli as happy (smiling) when they were holding a pen between their teeth compared to when they were not.

In Experiment 2, the stimuli are 11 images of a schematic hand whose gestures ranged from having all five fingers extended (they refer to the thumb as a finger) to having the little and the ring fingers curled (Figure 3.7). They expected that more of the hand images would be judged as having three fingers extended (thumb, index and middle finger) while opening and closing a pair of small scissors than when handling the large scissors.

1(b). What background or rationale is provided as justification for any hypothesis? Blaesi and Wilson provide a rather brief review of a selection of previous research in this area to justify their study (see the synopsis). They provide enough detail of this earlier work so the reader can see its relevance and its limitations. For example, they summarise studies on experts with specialised skills, such as professional sports players and dancers, and others who have taught people new movement sequences. They highlight confounds inherent in some of this earlier work, such as participants' expertise or choosing novel actions that confound the perception of action with the appreciation of rhythm.

They assert that none of these previous studies has shown a dynamic relationship whereby performing an action can affect the perception of another performing a similar action at the same time. They selected smiling and scissor-opening actions to circumvent the limitations perceived in the earlier work. They justify their choice as being ordinary, familiar actions requiring no special expertise. They hoped to have circumnavigated problems such as guessing the point of the study by telling participants the study was about their ability to multitask and simply asked their participants at the end what they thought the study was about. It is hard to be convinced that more people did not guess the purpose of either experiment and, nevertheless, simply reported back the instruction on multitasking.

They cite one study that used the pen tactic to make the participants smile without knowing that is what they were doing (Strack, Martin & Strepper, 1988), but provide no previous work to justify their choice of the scissor action.

2(a). Specify all the variables in the investigation and indicate what sort of variables they are (e.g. dependent vs. independent, manipulated, controlled, nuisance, confounding). Specify what level of measurement has been achieved for each dependent variable (nominal, ordinal, interval, ratio). Both experiments have one independent variable. In Experiment 1, it is 'pen': whether a pen was held between the participant's teeth or not on each trial. In Experiment 2, it is 'scissors': whether the participants opened and closed large or small scissors during each block of trials.

Blaesi and Wilson state their 11 face stimuli were used as an independent variable for the probit analyses,[3] which might be called 'emotional faces'. Presumably, their 11 hand stimuli were used as another independent variable for the probit analyses, which might be called 'hand extension'.

In Experiment 1, the dependent variable is the percentage of happy responses for each of the 11 faces that ranged from a frown to a smile. As each participant saw each image 15 times, the tally of how many times each face was judged to be happy could be turned into a percentage. The place on the face continuum that elicited the 50% happy response in each condition (pen and no pen) was calculated, for each observer, using a probit analysis.

In Experiment 2, the dependent variable is the percentage of 'three fingers extended' responses for the range of hand images. This is similarly the place on the hand extension continuum that elicited judgements that three fingers were extended on 50% of the trials for the two conditions (small or large scissors) using probit analyses. Both dependent variables are percentages, which are ratio data.

Pre-existing mood could be a nuisance variable in Experiment 1: if a participant was sad when they began the experiment, they may have judged more of the images as sad and, conversely, if they were happy at the start of the experiment, they may have judged more of the images as happy. It seems unlikely that their participants' general state of sadness or happiness would be affected according to whether they had a pen between their teeth or not, they would remain sad (or happy) wherever the pen was, so it is not a confound. Differences in general sadness or happiness would simply make the data from different people more varied.

Blaesi and Wilson cite studies that have reported that holding a pen between the teeth to approximate a smile can affect a person's emotional state, and emotional state can influence judgements of facial images. They are, therefore, suggesting that manipulated emotional state during the experiment could be a confound. In the studies they cite that have demonstrated such an effect, their participants held the pen between their teeth throughout the trials – that is, continuously (Strack et al., 1988; Soussignan, 2002; Ito et al., 2006). In the study by Blaesi and Wilson, however, the pen and no pen trials were alternated: for the act of smiling or not on consecutive trials to affect a person's emotional state would require their emotional state to fluctuate like a yo-yo. You could also wonder how much emotion may be evoked when repeatedly taking a pen in and out of your mouth in a laboratory setting (other than embarrassment).

2(b). Do the selected variables address the research hypothesis/hypotheses? The first independent variable, 'pen', addresses the research hypothesis that participants would judge more of the face stimuli as happy when they are holding a pen between their teeth, insofar as you are persuaded that holding a pen between your teeth is equivalent to smiling. Blaesi and Wilson cite other studies that have used this technique and found it to engage the same muscles. They describe the participants as placing the pen in their teeth horizontally, without the lips touching the pen. They do not say explicitly, but the cited studies have the pen protruding away from participants' noses, rather than lying parallel to their cheeks (Strack *et al.*, 1988). You can try it for yourself to see whether it engages the facial muscles in the same way as smiling or to the same extent.

Another question that can be raised about this technique is how many of the participants guessed the link between the pen action and the face displayed on screen. Three were excluded for reporting such a connection, but you could ask whether there were any more. Blaesi and Wilson depict three of the 11 face images (the endpoints, 'happy' and 'sad', and the midpoint, their image 6; see Figure 3.6 for the entire range). Image 6 was presumably meant to look neutral, and yet still displays quite a grimace. The only graph they presented was for one person, who, in the no-pen condition, judged image 6 as having a probability of being rated as a smile on over 70% of the trials, and, in the pen condition, judged it to be a smile on over 90% of the trials. It raises the concern that this participant, at least, may indeed have guessed the purpose of the study and, when asked if they had guessed, replied what they thought the authors wanted to hear, or else they had a strange idea of what a smile is. This is borne out in the average data: the 50% happy image is nearer to image 5 than image 6 (no pen condition: mean = 5.3, standard error (SE) = 0.18; pen condition: mean = 5.22, SE = 0.18).

Similarly, for Experiment 2, they provide images of the two endpoints (all digits extended or two fingers curled) and the midpoint, image 6 (see Figure 3.7 for the entire range). The sequence of the hand images for Experiment 2 is problematic: it would not take much finger curling to judge the hand as displaying two curled fingers and, indeed, this is borne out in their results – the 50% threshold for displaying two curled fingers was between scale positions 3 and 4, from a scale that ranged from 1 to 11 (large scissor condition: mean = 3.38, SE = 0.17; small scissor condition: mean = 3.73, SE = 0.21).

3. What did the participants have to do? (briefly) Is the study easily replicable? On each trial in Experiment 1, participants looked at a face from a series of 11 and had to decide whether the face was happy or sad. On alternate trials, they held a pen between their teeth. Participants initiated the trial themselves by a keypress; 500 milliseconds later a face was displayed for 750 milliseconds, and they had to judge whether the face had been happy or sad.

On each trial in Experiment 2, participants looked at a schematic hand from a series of 11 and had to decide whether the image had all five digits, or only the thumb and two fingers, extended. In alternate blocks of trials, they opened either a large or a small pair of scissors when a fixation point was displayed. An image appeared 750 milliseconds later that was displayed for 750 milliseconds, and they closed the scissors when the image was removed.

The authors mention participants were asked directly if they had guessed the point of the experiment. They did not mention whether the participants knew the experimenters: if they did, that may have affected their honesty. The participants (students) may have felt pressure to give expected answers. Indeed, only three were excluded from Experiment 1 for guessing the purpose of the experiment and none in Experiment 2.

While all of the images from each series are not presented, the methodology, trial by trial, is clear and could be replicated. Participant selection could not be replicated, as they did not give details of the students' average age, age range or gender.

4(a). What experimental design was used? Both experiments used a within-subjects, or repeated-measures design, as each student participated in both conditions in each experiment.

4(b). Do the method and design address the research hypothesis/ hypotheses? This question asks you for your point of view. Sometimes there is no right or wrong answer: it depends on your reading of the article and whether you are impressed with what was done. Personally, it is hard to be convinced that their students did not guess the purpose of the experiments, in which case the method and design do not address the research hypotheses. In addition, since the whole range of images in each experiment is not presented, there is no way to know whether the students' responses were sensible. It becomes clear when you can see the entire range (Emmorey, McCullough & Brentari, 2003; McCullough & Emery, 2009) (Figures 3.6 and 3.7). Judge for yourself if you think image 6 in Figure 3.6 looks neither happy nor sad; also judge if images 3/4 in Figure 3.7 show the cut-off between all digits extended or the little and ring fingers curled.

5. What comparisons were chosen for statistical analysis? The two conditions were compared in each experiment: having a pen or no pen between their teeth in Experiment 1 and opening or closing large or small scissors in Experiment 2.

6. What analysis was used? Was it appropriate? Few descriptive statistics are presented: for both experiments, Blaesi and Wilson present means and standard errors in the text. They present only one graph, showing the result for one participant for Experiment 1 (illustrated in Figure 3.8B). It would have been useful to have had a graph showing the average data for all, as illustrated in Figure 3.8A, rather than just the data from one participant. A sceptic may think they presented this participant's data as they showed the largest difference between the two conditions. This participant is certainly not representative of the average data.

A paired sample *t*-test was used in both experiments. The *t*-test is a parametric test used to compare two conditions. It assumes that the data are collected at the interval or ratio level, are normally distributed in each condition, and that there is homogeneity of variance across conditions. Although you could query the level of measurement that underlies the series of 11 images of faces, or the series of 11 images of hands, what is important is which data were compared in the analyses. They calculated, for each participant, the percentage of times that each face was judged to be happy and the percentage of times that the hand stimuli were judged to show three fingers extended. They then used a probit analysis for each participant to determine the image position on the scale from 'frowning' to 'smiling' that was judged to be happy on 50% of the trials. Similarly, they determined, for each observer, the image position on the scale that was judged to show the thumb and two fingers extended 50% of the time. Percentages yield ratio data. They then averaged these 50% scale positions across observers and compared these mean scores in each condition and in each experiment using two *t*-tests.

---

*Recap: There are four **'levels of measurement'** for data: nominal/categorical (you collect frequencies with this sort of data); ordinal (you can rank-order the numerical values of the data collected but the difference between scale points 1 and 2 is not the same as the difference between scale points 2 and 3, and so on for the length of the scale); interval (here the size of the numerical difference between successive scale points is equal, but there is no true zero). The fourth type of data is ratio, where the difference between successive scale points is equal and there is a true zero. See Chapter 2 for further elaboration.*

Blaesi and Wilson do not mention whether they undertook tests for normality of their data in each condition and in each experiment. As mentioned in Chapter 2, there are tests for normality, for example, the Kolmogorov-Smirnov test. They do not mention whether they had homogeneity of variance. Both normality and homogeneity of variance are required to conduct parametric paired-sample *t*-tests. They do, however, present means and standard errors in the text for each condition in each experiment. The standard error is a measure of variability in the data; it is the standard deviation divided by the square root of the sample size minus one, so you can easily go from one to the other. The standard

Figure 3.9 The average data for Experiment 1, together with standard error bars. When authors choose to display their data graphically, the scale of the ordinate, or y-axis, is up to them. They seldom show the entire range of possible scores (A), as the condition differences are hard to see. Instead, they tend to choose a range to maximise the impression of differences between the conditions (B). In (C) the range has been extended so that the data from that one participant could be included, marked by asterisks. Each graph gives an entirely different impression of the data.

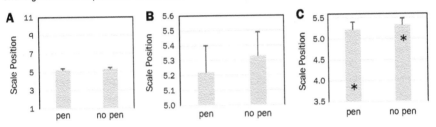

deviation is the square root of the variance. You can turn a standard error into a standard deviation and then square it to obtain the variance. For homogeneity of variance, you want the variance to be comparable in size in each condition. As mentioned in Chapter 2, general guidance is that the largest variance should be no more than three times the variance of the smallest. In this article, this condition holds.

As mentioned, Blaesi and Wilson do not provide graphs showing the average data in each condition with standard error bars. It is always easier to compare the data from different conditions visually, so the lack of relevant graphs is certainly an omission. An example for Experiment 1 is provided in Figure 3.9.

Blaesi and Wilson also do not comment on outliers, nor did they provide effect sizes. The data for the one person who had a difference score of over one scale point suggests at least one outlier (Figure 3.8B). To appreciate this, consider how the data would appear had they provided a graph of their average data instead of just the curves fitted to the group's data. Figure 3.9 illustrates three possible options. The choice of range along the ordinate, or y-axis, is up to the authors. They would be unlikely to present Figure 3.9A, where the ordinate covers all 11 scale points, as this masks the differences between conditions. They would be more likely to present Figure 3.9B, with a reduced range along the ordinate to maximise the impression of differences between the conditions. If the range is extended to allow the data from that one participant to be indicated, you can readily appreciate how far that participant was from the group average in the pen condition (Figure 3.9C).

So, were the analyses appropriate? On the face of it, *t*-tests were appropriate for the type of data analysed, but it is impossible to tell if the analyses Blaesi and Wilson performed were appropriate due to missing details showing whether their data met the assumptions for parametric tests.

7. What was the main result? In Experiment 1, Blaesi and Wilson's participants had lower thresholds to perceive a happy face when they themselves were smiling or holding a pen in their mouth.

Cohen's d is a measure of effect size and can be calculated from the t statistic provided ($t = 2.35$) and the square root of the sample size.[4] Cohen provided a rule of thumb to judge the magnitude of effect sizes: small is 0.2, medium is 0.5, large is 0.8. The effect size for Experiment 1 is 4.7: nearly a medium effect size despite first impressions given by simply reporting means and standard errors for each condition. It is always a good idea to calculate effect sizes rather than simply presenting means, standard errors and significance values, particularly when the mean differences between conditions appears small (scale points 5.22 and 5.33, one-tenth of a scale point). The effect size gives an idea of how meaningful a significant difference is.

In Experiment 2, the participants had lower thresholds to perceive the schematic hand as having three extended fingers when they were simultaneously opening and closing the small scissors than when handling the large ones. Again, the size of the difference between the conditions appears small (3.38 and 3.73 for the small and large scissor conditions, respectively, a difference of 0.35 of a scale point). Nevertheless, the effect size can be worked out to be 5.7: a medium effect size.

Effect sizes of 4.7 and 5.7 indicate the group difference in both experiments, even if small, are sound.

8. What conclusions were drawn? Were they valid? Blaesi and Wilson conclude that their studies support a bi-directional account of the mirror system: what we see can affect our actions and our actions can affect what we see. They suggest there may be a common neural code involved in seeing another's action and performing the same action yourself. Bi-directional effects are consistent with these suggestions, but the authors provide no direct evidence that the mirror system is involved at all – at best their results are consistent with the mirror system being involved. They try to tie their study to more mainstream accounts of the mirror system's involvement in imitation by mentioning that it contributes to social empathy and social interaction. This is largely irrelevant to their own study. They further speculate that the mirror system may be providing top-down support for visual perception, making it faster, more fluent and *more* accurate (Blaesi & Wilson, 2010, p. 309). Increased accuracy is not what this study has assessed, however: their participants were arguably *less* accurate if what they were doing influenced what they saw. They cite only one reference that other top-down effects can speed up perception, and that is a study specifically on time delays: applying it to the situation employed in their tasks is equally irrelevant. There is little discussion of their actual data and a lot of speculation beyond what their data justified.

9. What are your main criticisms of the report? This question is for you to consider. Although the group differences in each experiment may have been statistically significant and associated with reasonable effect sizes, they were small. You could ask yourself how compelling the evidence really is. Other key issues I would include (although by all means disagree) would be that Experiment 1 is the more problematic of the two. Not only is embarrassment likely to be involved, putting a pen in and out of your mouth on 330 consecutive trials would have taken some time, as well as being unhygienic. Blaesi and Wilson do not mention how long their experiments took. You may also feel foolish opening and closing a pair of scissors on 330 trials. Other issues include:

1 The sparse stimuli presentation – it would have been useful to see the entire range of 11 images for each experiment.
2 The sparse data presentation – the lack of an overall graph for both experiments.
3 Presenting means and standard errors in the text rather than graphically.
4 The statistical treatment of the results – there was no discussion whether the data met the assumptions for t-tests.
5 No discussion of outliers, despite clearly having at least one.
6 The very real chance that participants did indeed guess the purpose of the experiment and some at least gave responses they thought the experimenter was looking for.
7 The lack of participant details (males, females, mean age and age range).
8 Not being told if the experimenter was known to the participants, i.e. a lecturer or tutor of the students.
9 Not screening the participants for their own mood at the time they completed Experiment 1, or afterwards. Blaesi and Wilson suggest that the emotional state of the participant might have been manipulated in their results, which 'justifies' Experiment 2. It would have been fairly simple to assess this.
10 If they thought their participants' emotional state might have been manipulated during Experiment 1, you could wonder why they used faces in the first place.
11 Muscle fatigue in Experiment 2 may well have been a nuisance variable, as their participants' hands would tire opening and closing scissors 330 times.

These issues compromise both the internal and external validity of the study.

10. What are the main strengths of the report? The fact that perception can affect action is well known, but it was an interesting idea to turn this issue around using familiar actions rather than novel ones, as used in previous studies, which required participants to undergo prior training. Another strength is that both experiments produced differences between the two conditions that were consistent with their hypothesis that action would influence perception.

Exercises

1 Discuss whether the authors have provided a firm foundation for their study. What is novel that they hoped to bring to this area of research? How natural-istic were the tasks selected? Comment on whether the authors dealt satis-factorily with the possibility that their participants guessed the point of their study.

2 What analyses were performed? Were the analyses suitable for their research question(s)? The authors conclude that they have shown that the mirror-neuron system can indeed yield bi-directional effects on perception: what we see can affect our actions and our actions can affect what we see. Are their claims persuasive, given the stimuli and analyses that they used?

Notes

1 See https://www.youtube.com/watch?v=sxwn1w7MJvk for a demonstration of the effect.
2 This action was first described as a technique to make people smile by Strack, Martin and Strepper (1988). See https://replicationindex.com/category/pen-in-mouth-para-digm/ for an image.
3 A probit analysis involves fitting percentage data with a sigmoid, or S-shaped, curve. The image position corresponding to 50% happy or three fingers extended can then be identified for each participant. See Figure 3.8.
4 Cohen's d for a paired-sample t-test can be calculated as the t value divided by the square root of the sample size. This statistic tells you the difference between two sample means as d standard deviation units from zero, giving you an idea of the mag-nitude of the difference between the two sample means.

References

Armel, K. C., & Ramachandran, V. S. (2003). Projecting sensations to external objects: Evidence from skin conductance response. *Proceedings of the Royal Society B: Bio-logical Sciences, 270*(1523), 1499–1506. https://doi.org/10.1098/rspb.2003.2364.

Blaesi, S., & Wilson, M. (2010). The mirror reflects both ways: Action influences percep-tion of others. *Brain and Cognition, 72*(2), 306–309. https://doi.org/10.1016/j.bandc.2009.10.001.

Botvinick, M., & Cohen, J. (1998). Rubber hands 'feel' touch that eyes see. *Nature, 391*(6669), 756. https://doi.org/10.1038/35784.

Braun, N., Debener, S., Spychala, N. *et al.* (2018). The senses of agency and ownership: A review. *Frontiers in Psychology, 9,* 535. https://doi.org/10.3389/fpsyg.2018.00535.

Calvo-Merino, B., Glaser, D. E., Grèzes, J. *et al.* (2005). Action observation and acquired motor skills: An fMRI study with expert dancers. *Cerebral Cortex, 15*(8), 1243–1249. https://doi.org/10.1093/cercor/bhi007.

Calvo-Merino, B., Grèzes, J., Glaser, D. E. *et al.* (2006). Seeing or doing? Influence of visual and motor familiarity in action observation. *Current Biology, 16*(19), 1905–1910. https://doi.org/10.1016/j.cub.2006.07.065.

Casile, A., & Giese, M. A. (2006). Nonvisual motor training influences biological motion perception. *Current Biology, 16*(1), 69–74. https://doi.org/10.1016/j.cub.2005.10.071.

Chan, B. L., Witt, R., Charrow, A. P. *et al.* (2007). Mirror therapy in phantom limb pain. *New England Journal of Medicine, 357*(21), 2206–2207. https://doi.org/10.1056/NEJMc071927.

Costantini, M., & Haggard, P. (2007). The rubber hand illusion: Sensitivity and reference frame for body ownership. *Consciousness and Cognition, 16*(2), 229–240. https://doi.org/10.1016/j.concog.2007.01.001.

Derryberry, D., & Reed, M. A. (2002). Anxiety-related attentional biases and their regulation by attentional control. *Journal of Abnormal Psychology, 111*(2), 225–236. https://doi.org/10.1037/0021-843X.111.2.225.

Emmorey, K., McCullough, S., & Brentari, D. (2003). Categorical perception in American Sign Language. *Language and Cognitive Processes, 18*(1), 21–45. https://doi.org/10.1080/01690960143000416.

Guenther, K. (2016). 'It's all done with mirrors': V.S. Ramachandran and the material culture of phantom limb research. *Medical History, 60*(3), 342–358. https://doi.org/10.1017/mdh.2016.27.

Ito, T. A., Chiao, K. W., Devine, P. G. *et al.* (2006). The influence of facial feedback on race bias. *Psychological Science, 17*(3), 256–261. https://doi.org/10.1111/j.1467-9280.2006.01694.x.

Kalckert, A. (2018). Commentary: Switching to the rubber hand. *Frontiers in Psychology, 9,* 588. https://doi.org/10.3389/fpsyg.2018.00588.

Lloyd, D. M. (2007). Spatial limits on referred touch to an alien limb may reflect boundaries of visuo-tactile peripersonal space surrounding the hand. *Brain and Cognition, 64*(1), 104–109. https://doi.org/10.1016/j.bandc.2006.09.013.

McCullough, S., & Emery, K. (2009). Categorical perception of affective and linguistic facial expressions. *Cognition, 110*(2), 208–221. https://doi.org/10.1016/j.cognition.2008.11.007.

Paradis, M. (2006). More belles infidèles – or why do so many bilingual studies speak with forked tongue? *Journal of Neurolinguistics, 19*(3), 195–208. https://doi.org/10.1016/j.jneuroling.2005.11.002.

Ramachandran, V. S., & Rodgers-Ramachandran, D. (1996). Synaesthesia in phantom limbs induced with mirrors. *Proceedings of the Royal Society B: Biological Sciences, 263*(1369), 377–386. https://doi.org/10.1098/rspb.1996.0058.

Rizzolatti, G., & Craighero, L. (2004). The mirror-neuron system. *Annual Review of Neuroscience, 27,* 169–192. doi: 10.1146/annurev.neuro.27.070203.144230.

Robertson, I. H., Manly, T., Andrade, J. *et al.* (1997). 'Oops!': Performance correlates of everyday attentional failures in traumatic brain injured and normal subjects. *Neuropsychologia, 35*(6), 747–758. https://doi.org/10.1016/S0028-3932(97)00015-8.

Simon, J. R. (1969). Reactions toward the source of stimulation. *Journal of Experimental Psychology, 81*(1), 174–176. https://doi.org/10.1037/h0027448.

Simon, J. R., & Rudell, A. P. (1967). Auditory S-R compatibility: The effect of an irrelevant cue on information processing. *Journal of Applied Psychology, 51*(3), 300–304. https://doi.org/10.1037/h0020586.

Soussignan, R. (2002). Duchenne smile, emotional experience, and autonomic reactivity. A test of the facial feedback hypothesis. *Emotion, 2*(1), 52–74. https://doi.org/10.1037/1528-3542.2.1.52.

Strack, F., Martin, L., & Stepper, S. (1988). Inhibiting and facilitating conditions of the human smile: A nonobtrusive test of the facial feedback hypothesis. *Journal of Personality and Social Psychology, 54*(5), 768–777. https://doi.org/10.1037/0022-3514.54.5.768.

Tsakiris, M. (2010). My body in the brain: A neurocognitive model of body-ownership. *Neuropsychologia, 48*(3), 703–712. https://doi.org/10.1016/j.neuropsychologia.2009.09.034.

Tsakiris, M. (2011). The sense of body ownership, in S. Gallagher (ed.) *The Oxford Handbook of the Self.* Oxford: Oxford University Press, pp. 180–203.

Tsakiris, M. (2017). The multisensory basis of the self: From body to identity to others. *Quarterly Journal of Experimental Psychology, 70*(4), 597–609. https://doi.org/10.1080/17470218.2016.1181768.

Yeh, S.-L., Lane, T.J., Chang, A.-Y., & Chien, S.-E. (2017). Switching to the rubber hand. *Frontiers in Psychology, 8*, 2172. https://doi.org/10.3389/fpsyg.2017.02172.

4   The dark triad

In this chapter, we will discuss two articles that investigate personality traits known as the dark triad: Machiavellianism, psychopathy and narcissism. While intuitively these terms may appear distinct, there is a large body of research that has explored how much they overlap. There is an enduring appeal in this research area: a fascination to understand a person's malevolence and their motives on the one hand, and the impact these personalities have in personal relationships and in wider society on the other.

The *Oxford English Dictionary* defines a Machiavellian as someone who is cunning, scheming and unscrupulous. It comes from a sixteenth-century book on political philosophy by Machiavelli, which describes a ruthless approach when treating others in order to further one's own self-interests and ambitions. Psychopaths are sometimes portrayed as exhibiting unrelenting aggressive, impulsive and violent social behaviours, but they can also be charming while emotionally cold. Narcissus, in Greek mythology, is a beautiful and arrogant young man who spurned the approaches of others yet fell in love with his own reflection in a pool of water. These personalities are often portrayed (parodied?) in books, films and plays as the character we like to dislike, particularly when they eventually meet their demise.

Most of you will have seen the film, or read the book, *The Silence of the Lambs* (Harris, 1988), which describes the relationship between Hannibal Lecter (a serial killing, cannibalistic, former psychiatrist) and Clarice Starling (a trainee psychologist at the FBI). Lecter personifies the 'evil genius' sometimes associated with psychopathy, yet he arguably also displays Machiavellian and narcissistic traits. It is a good film, and I do not expect it to pop up in an academic article but, for general awareness, it is an apt example. Lecter is an extreme, fictional, character: closer to home there are all too frequent reports in the news of horrendous murders, people who keep bodies in their freezers or in their garden, kidnappings involving torture or torment, or apparently unprovoked violent attacks on individuals or on the many. Even closer to home, we all know people who can be manipulative, self-centred and/or callous. Do these people need to be intelligent to manipulate those around them, to be ruthless in pursuit of their own goals, or to mask their true selves so they can get on in a society that they hold in disdain? Kowalski *et al.* (2018) consider that this question is still open to debate.

There is also an interest in being able to recognise dark personalities: if there are clues in the demeanour or behaviours of someone that could alert us to an underlying, less appealing side to their character, we may then choose to avoid them, or at least not form close relationships, whether that be personal or professional. Rauthmann and Kolar (2013) consider the attractiveness of Machiavellians, psychopaths and narcissists in the context of choosing them as a friend, liking them or perhaps seeing them as a short- or long-term partner.

Research in this area raises immediate ethical issues, as often the experimenter must be deceitful about their research to get participants to let their guard down and be honest about their thoughts and motivations. Judge for yourself whether the authors in this chapter have succeeded. For generalisability, there may be a question at the back of our minds whether there is a continuum, with everyone having the odd antisocial or self-serving impulse. By studying the dark triad, we may get insights into components of everyone's behaviour, perhaps including our own. This is certainly the reasoning behind these articles, since the authors tested lay people, not people from a psychiatric clinic.

> **Kowalski, C. M., Kwiatkowska, K., Kwiatkowska, M. M., Ponikiewska, K., Rogoza, R., & Schermer, J. A. (2018). The Dark Triad traits and intelligence: Machiavellians are bright, and narcissists and psychopaths are ordinary.** *Personality and Individual Differences, 135,* 1–6. https://doi.org/10.1016/j.paid.2018.06.049.

Kowalski *et al.* (2018) consider that the question of a relationship between intelligence and the dark triad personalities is still open to debate, as previous studies have not adequately considered different types of intelligence. They maintain that previous studies have assessed crystallised intelligence rather than fluid intelligence. Crystallised intelligence stems from knowledge that has been learned or acquired from experience. Using language and reading are examples of using crystallised intelligence. Fluid intelligence is akin to problem-solving: it does not depend on having learnt something or acquired a skill; it relates instead to formulating relationships between items and abstract reasoning. If you have a new problem to solve and you cannot rely on what you know or what you have previously learned, you need to create new associations to solve the problem, which uses fluid intelligence. Kowalski *et al.* wish to extend previous research by examining fluid rather than crystallised intelligence.

Synopsis

Introduction

Kowalski *et al.* (2018) begin with a lengthy section defining the personalities of the dark triad. They cite several studies that question whether the dark triad describes three distinct personality types: some research has proposed, instead, that Machiavellianism can be construed as a component of psychopathy. Both personality types, for example, exhibit low self-control and high impulsivity. They later cite a study, however, which describes Machiavellians as having superior impulse control. They emphasise that theoretical accounts of the dark triad portray them as distinct personalities, whereas empirical studies paint a rather more mixed picture. There are reports of differences in cheating and lying between psychopaths and Machiavellians, for example, but no association between general intelligence or general mental ability and the three dark triad personalities. The authors criticise some studies that used self-ratings of intelligence, and others that examined either general or crystallised intelligence. They comment that fluid intelligence should be assessed instead, as it is more relevant to the scheming, manipulative, self-serving traits of the dark triad.

Methods

Kowalski *et al.* tested 128 high school students in Poland. They completed a number of questionnaires, although they do not say how many or what they all were, but they did include the Short Dark Triad Questionnaire (SDT; Jones & Paulhus, 2014), translated into Polish and, two weeks later, the classic version of Raven's Standard Progressive Matrices (SPM; Raven, 1981). The SDT contains 27 questions, nine for each of the dark triad personalities. Examples include *You should wait for the right time to get back at people* (Machiavellian), *I have been compared to famous people* (narcissist), and *People who mess with me always regret it* (psychopath). The SPM comprises 60 problem-solving tests, each of which involves a sequence of geometric designs that increase in complexity. The final piece of each sequence is missing. The task is to identify the pattern or rule that connects the elements of each sequence and then select the correct design from a number of possible alternatives to complete the sequence. Task difficulty increases from the first to the last sets of designs. It is taken as a measure of non-verbal, fluid intelligence. Many examples can be found if you look up Raven's progressive matrices on the internet.

Results

Kowalski *et al.* report that the participants' Machiavellian ratings from the SDT were significantly higher than their narcissism or psychopathy ratings, and that the narcissism ratings were significantly higher than the psychopathy ratings (three paired-sample *t*-tests).

Kowalski et al. then use structural equation modelling (SEM) to test for relationships between intelligence, as assessed by Raven's SPM, and the three dark triad personalities. In SEM, a network model is defined based on theory and/or prior research and the data are tested against that model to determine how well it fits, or explains, the data. Analysis of variance (ANOVA), multiple regression and factor analysis are specialised types of SEM, but do not assume an underlying causality (Bollen & Noble, 2011).

Kowalski *et al.* created a model to determine how well scores on Raven's SPM predict ratings for Machiavellianism, psychopathy and narcissism. They report their model provided a good fit to their data (see GQ6 for a schematic of their model). They first report that the three dark triad personalities were all positively intercorrelated. The highest correlation was between Machiavellianism and psychopathy. They further report that fluid intelligence only predicted the Machiavellian ratings. Their model, however, explained only a negligible amount of the variance in the fluid intelligence scores. To confirm the link between fluid intelligence and Machiavellianism, Kowalski *et al.* created low and high intelligence groups by selecting only those students who lay in the top one-third of Raven's SPM scores and those who lay in the lowest third. They then compared Machiavellian, psychopathy and narcissism ratings for these low and high intelligence groups (three independent-samples *t*-tests) and also correlated the ratings for each dark triad trait and intelligence. They found again significant results only for the Machiavellian ratings: the high intelligence group scored significantly higher on Machiavellianism than the low intelligence group, and there was a significant positive association between Machiavellian ratings and intelligence scores (presumably Pearson's *r*).

Conclusions

Kowalski *et al.* spend a large part of their discussion repeating their view that previous research has shown little association between Machiavellianism and intelligence because they assessed crystallised, rather than fluid, intelligence. They repeat that theoretical accounts imply there should be a relationship between intelligence and Machiavellianism, as Machiavellians are supposed to be skilled manipulators and strategic planners. They conclude that their study shows that fluid intelligence does indeed predict Machiavellian ratings, and suggest this reflects skill in abstract thinking, strategic thinking and planning. They consider that they have provided support for a description of a Machiavellian as an evil genius. Their finding that narcissism was not associated with *fluid* intelligence adds to prior research that found no association between narcissism and *crystallised* intelligence.

On psychopathy, Kowalski *et al.* are ambivalent. They suggest their results are possibly consistent with prior work that has found a negative association between psychopathy and crystallised intelligence, but cite other work that has found no such association. They suggest further research is needed, since their study had a modest sample size and, on average, their students scored more highly on fluid intelligence than the norms for Raven's SPM scores in the Polish population. They further suggest that assessments of fluid intelligence in psychopathy need also to include an assessment of impulsivity, as that could affect the amount of effort they are prepared to put in to solving problems. It is not clear why this concern was not addressed in their own study, rather than introduced as an afterthought in the Discussion. Their students did, after all, complete a number of questionnaires during the first session (we are not told why or which ones), so an impulsivity assessment could also have been included (see, for example, the standard impulsivity scale developed by Patton, Stanford & Barratt, 1995). They end with comments on limitations: the modest sample size for studies of this type, their use of the short dark triad questionnaire rather than the full-length version, the restricted age range of their participants and the high proportion of females. They do not cite prevalence rates for different age groups from existing literature, or comment on the preponderance of dark personality traits that has been reported for males rather than females. Instead, they recommend caution when interpreting the results from their study and encourage further research on different populations.

The ten general questions (10GQs)

When this article has been discussed in class, common stumbling blocks have included levels of measurement, assumptions behind the use of parametric tests, different experimental designs, the difference between experimental design and the statistical analyses and, inevitably, structural equation modelling. It is a good idea to brush up on these issues before tackling this article.

1(a). Does the report specify an hypothesis? If so, what is it? Is there more than one? Kowalski *et al.* have three hypotheses related to fluid intelligence: one directional and two that predict a null hypothesis: (1) there will be an association between Machiavellianism and fluid intelligence – those who have high Machiavellian scores will have high fluid intelligence scores, whereas scores for (2) psychopaths and (3) narcissists will be unrelated to fluid intelligence. It is never a good idea to predict a null hypothesis: if the data do indeed show no statistically significant association between scores on psychopathy or narcissism scales and a measure of fluid intelligence, it is impossible to know if that has occurred because there is no association or because no association was demonstrated with the measures and sample used. There may be an association, but it could be that the way the constructs of psychopathy, narcissism and/or fluid intelligence were measured was inappropriate or insensitive, the sample was inappropriate, or both.

Although no hypotheses were stated, Kowalski *et al.* performed three paired-sample *t*-tests to compare the Machiavellian, psychopathy and narcissism ratings, so they must have had hypothesised that at least one of the traits is more prevalent in their sample than the other two. That is, Machiavellian ratings may be higher or lower than narcissism or psychopathy ratings, and/or narcissism ratings may be higher or lower than the ratings of psychopathy. These were presumably bi-directional, given their review of mixed findings in prior literature.

1(b). What background or rationale is provided as justification for any hypothesis? Rather bizarrely, Kowalski *et al.* begin their Introduction with a characterisation of the three personalities using a cartoon character, the Unabomber and Dracula (Vlad the Impaler), and describe this as a theoretical narrative. They then focus mainly on Machiavellianism and psychopathy and cite literature that has shown both similarities and differences between them. They review studies on intelligence and the dark triad, which have provided mixed results. Generally, Machiavellians appear to stand apart from psychopaths and narcissists. For example, they contrast studies that have used self-ratings of intelligence with those that have used more objective measures. Narcissists, and sometime psychopaths, overrate their own intelligence, whereas Machiavellians do not. They report that few associations have been found between the dark triad personalities and objective measures of general intelligence or cognitive ability.

The discussion of the differences and similarities between Machiavellians and psychopaths is lengthy and repetitive, and at times also unedifying. For example, they cite a study 'where psychopaths, but not Machiavellians, cheated in coin-flip tasks when there was a serious risk of punishment; when ego-depleted, however, the results for the Machiavellian individuals were similar to those of the psychopaths' (2018, p. 2). Bearing in mind that dark personalities are also described as high sensation-seeking and easily bored individuals, how motivated would they be when asked to participate in a coin-flip task? What could be a serious punishment? How was ego-depletion accomplished? On the face of it, this study appears to have little external validity. Presenting a study that used a trivial task, where the results initially support the distinction between Machiavellians and psychopaths, and then do not, muddies rather than clarifies the argument on whether Machiavellians differ from psychopaths.

They cite other research that supports Machiavellianism and psychopathy as distinct traits. For example, when psychopaths and Machiavellians are unfaithful to their partners, the relationships with the psychopaths tend to disintegrate, whereas the relationships with Machiavellians tend to survive. A possible explanation is that the psychopaths are reckless whereas Machiavellians are more calculating and put more effort into manipulating their partner to stay together. The premise Kowalski *et al.* adopt is: if Machiavellians put more intellectual effort into their deceptions and lying, perhaps they are more intellectually flexible in general? To justify their hypothesis, that Machiavellians will score highly on fluid intelligence, whereas psychopaths and narcissists will not, they rely in large part on the lay caricature of Machiavellians as particularly adept schemers.

The contribution Kowalski *et al.* hope to make to this area of research is to assess fluid intelligence using an objective measure, as fluid intelligence is more relevant to the scheming, manipulative, self-serving traits of the dark triad personalities than measures of either crystallised or general intelligence. They say they base their hypothesis that singles out Machiavellians on both empirical and theoretical considerations, but the empirical work cited does not lead to a directional hypothesis. They acknowledge that they are predicting a null relationship between psychopathy or narcissism and fluid intelligence, but they do not comment that this is ordinarily deprecated.

Separate to the hypotheses regarding fluid intelligence, they also conduct pairwise comparisons of the ratings of the three personality types to assess whether any of the ratings for each personality type differ from the other two. A significant difference from one of these comparisons would indicate that one of the dark traits is more prevalent than the other. For example, if there are more high ratings for Machiavellianism than for narcissism, and the difference was significant, that indicates there are more Machiavellians than narcissists in their sample: if you are a Machiavellian, you are unlikely to be a narcissist.

Kowalski *et al.*, however, provide no background on prevalence rates of Machiavellianism, psychopathy or narcissism in the general population. They cite no prior research or theoretical arguments to expect one of the dark personalities to be more or less prevalent than the other two. They also do not provide information on whether these personality traits are stable characteristics from childhood, or whether they begin to emerge and differentiate during adolescence, or whether there is a peak age when they manifest themselves most completely. Given that they only tested teenagers, this is a fairly serious omission that limits the external validity, and thereby the generalisability, of their work. There are a few studies on the developmental trajectory of dark personalities that have suggested they peak in adolescence and early adulthood (for a review, see Klimstra *et al.*, 2020). It would be interesting to know whether the average ratings obtained for each personality type are similar to those reported in previous studies, as then you would be reassured that the data that have been collected are valid.

Kowalski *et al.* also suggest their study should shed light on the question of whether Machiavellians are particularly good at manipulation because of greater fluid intelligence or simply greater impulse control (Jones & Paulhus, 1990). This is mentioned in the Introduction, but not picked up again in the discussion of their results. Since they did not assess impulse control, this suggestion is beside the point.

2(a). Specify all the variables in the investigation and indicate what sort of variables they are (e.g. dependent vs. independent, manipulated, controlled, nuisance, confounding). Specify what level of measurement has been achieved for each dependent variable (nominal, ordinal, interval, ratio). There is one conceptual independent variable: dark triad status, as Kowalski *et al.* chose to study these personality traits. They could have chosen impulsivity or sadism, but they did not, they chose Machiavellianism, psychopathy and narcissism.

Kowalski *et al.* use structural equation modelling (SEM) to explore whether fluid intelligence predicts each personality type. Although no variables have been manipulated, in SEM the independent variable is the predictor variable, in this case, the latent variable fluid intelligence as encapsulated by Raven's SPM. It may seem curious to consider level of measurement for an independent variable, but the term independent is a label for the predictor variable, and it consists of measured data. Data from Raven's SPM are arguably ratio as there is a true zero: should someone get all of the items wrong, it implies they have no ability to demonstrate the concept of fluid intelligence as it is represented by Raven's SPM. A different test of fluid intelligence may show that they do have an appreciation of abstract reasoning or problem-solving, it is just not captured by Raven's SPM. For the correlations and t-tests, fluid intelligence is a dependent variable.

The SDT is also a dependent variable. Its 27 questions are measured on 5-point Likert scales with endpoints 'strongly agree' and 'strongly disagree', coded as 1 to 5. Rating scales with these endpoints are often considered interval data (hardliners will insist the data from such scales are only ordinal; see Chapter 2).

Kowalski *et al.* do not mention any controlled variables, although age could be considered controlled since the students were all a similar age (16–18 years).[1] They do not mention if there were any exclusion criteria. There were two test sessions: during one, they completed a series of questionnaires including the SDT, in the other, they completed Raven's matrices. A nuisance variable may be tiredness or boredom in the first session: Kowalski *et al.* do not say how many questionnaires were administered, or how long they took to complete. We also are not told whether the questionnaires administered in the first session were administered in the same order: if they were, tiredness or boredom may have affected their responses to the questions completed towards the end of the session. We are not told where in the battery of questionnaires the SDT appeared.

The students took between 25 and 55 minutes to complete the second session. A possible nuisance variable could be termed frame of mind. If the students who completed Raven's SPM quickly were left in the classroom waiting for the slower students to finish, were they then chatting with students near to them or fidgeting, or did they leave the classroom? Thirty minutes is a long time to expect teenagers to sit quietly. Whatever the students did who finished quickly could make the slower students flustered and so they may have rushed to complete the harder SPM items, as they are presented at the end of the test booklet.

2(b). Do the selected variables address the research hypothesis/ hypotheses? Raven's SPM is a standard test that is routinely used to assess at least one aspect of non-verbal, fluid intelligence and thereby does address the hypotheses regarding fluid intelligence.

The SDT is an established questionnaire, with over 1,100 citations in 2020. It comprises 27 questions divided between three subscales, one for each of the dark triad personalities. Kowalski *et al.* quote reliability coefficients for their sample that are greater than 0.7 for each subscale (Cronbach's alpha: 0.71 for narcissism and 0.78 for both Machiavellianism and psychopathy[2]). This questionnaire is appropriate as a way to assess

Machiavellianism, narcissism and psychopathy, although it has been criticised for not adequately differentiating between Machiavellianism and
psychopathy (Persson, Kajonius & Garcia, 2019). (For a review of alternative questionnaires, see Furnham *et al.*, 2014.)

One issue with the SDT, however, is its appropriateness for use with
mostly 16-year-olds. Items on the psychopathy scale include, for example, *I enjoy having sex with people I hardly know* and *I have never gotten
into trouble with the law* (these are reverse coded when it comes to combining the scales, so 'strongly agree' becomes 'strongly disagree' and so
on for the five scale categories). These questions may be a little early for
some of their students. A second issue is who administered it: if the questionnaires were handed out by the students' teachers, that may have
influenced how truthful their responses would be. The students may be
concerned that they could be identified, or they may think it amusing to
depict a maverick personality, perhaps to see the effect it had on their
teacher when later they were (presumably) debriefed. They may tend to
brag or boast so they can show off with their peers later on, rather than
respond truthfully. Sixteen and 17 are peculiar ages and different students are at different stages of maturity.

3. What did the participants have to do? (briefly) Is the study easily replicable?
Kowalski *et al.* tested 128 high school students
during class at two time points: at the start of term they completed
several questionnaires including the SDT; then, two weeks later, they
completed the classic version of Raven's SPM. They do not say how
many questionnaires were completed in the first session, or how long
they took to complete. Raven's SPM took between 25 and 55 minutes to
complete.

Kowalski *et al.* also do not say how many students were tested simultaneously: in their data file it appears that the students were allocated
into three groups to complete Raven's SPM. It seems likely that the three
groups were three different classes. We do not know if the groups were
tested in parallel: if they were not, then there is a chance of diffusion of
information between the groups when the students tested first met with
the others and talked about what they had been asked to do.

The study is partly replicable: since we do not know how many questionnaires were completed, in what order they were completed, how long
they took to complete, or whether all 128 students were tested simultaneously, session 1 cannot be replicated in its entirety.

Another issue related to replicability is that we do not know what the
students were told about the study before each session started. It is usual
to give a little introduction at the start of an experimental session, so that
the participants know what to expect and why they are being asked to
participate. Without that, they cannot give consent to participate. Kowalski *et al.* mention consent was obtained from the students' parents, the
headmaster and the teachers, but they do not detail what was consented

to and we do not know what was then relayed to the students prior to the test sessions. This may have affected the students' motivation when participating.

We also do not know the layout of the classroom and whether the students were seated sufficiently closely to be able to view their neighbour's responses. Since people with dark triad personalities are known to lie and cheat, they may well have looked to see what their neighbour's answers were before filling in the answers for themselves, particularly for Raven's SPM. Cheating could be a confounding variable if those who scored highly on dark triad ratings cheated more than those with lower dark triad ratings. Testing large numbers in classes is not uncommon, but it brings with it a lack of control over each participant's behaviour.

Kowalski *et al.* also do not mention whether they included any assessment of their students' tendency to provide socially desirable answers, despite flagging this as a trait exhibited by both narcissists and Machiavellians in their Introduction. There is, for example, a social desirability scale that could have been included (Crowne & Marlowe, 1960). If the results show similar associations between fluid intelligence and both Machiavellianism and narcissism, the desire to provide socially desirable answers on the SDT would be a confounding variable, as it cuts across both personality types. Fortunately for Kowalski *et al.*, in the Results section the associations between fluid intelligence and Machiavellianism or narcissism do differ.

4(a). What experimental design was used? The experimental design is correlational: Kowalski *et al.* are testing for a network of associations between intelligence and the three dark triad personalities. To compare ratings across the dark triad (the paired-sample *t*-tests), they make use of a repeated-measures component inherent in the correlational design.

4(b). Do the method and design address the research hypothesis/ hypotheses? Broadly, the method and design do address the research hypotheses but, given the caveats presented above concerning the appropriateness of some of the SDT questions for teenagers and the lack of information on the testing session, the method could have been more tightly controlled.

5. What comparisons were chosen for statistical analysis? Kowalski *et al.* first compared SDT scores for Machiavellianism vs. psychopathy, Machiavellianism vs. narcissism and psychopathy vs. narcissism. They then compared associations between fluid intelligence, as measured by Raven's SPM, and Machiavellianism, psychopathy and narcissism using SEM. Finally, for each group, they selected the third of the participants with the lowest Raven's SPM scores and the third with the highest to create subgroups of lower and higher scorers, and then compared the SDT scores between those subgroups. They also performed three correlations using the data from these low and high Raven's SPM subgroups and their Machiavellianism, psychopathy and narcissism ratings.

6. What analysis was used? Was it appropriate? Kowalski *et al.* first performed three paired-sample *t*-tests, which indicated that Machiavellianism ratings were significantly higher than ratings on psychopathy or narcissism, and narcissism ratings were significantly higher than those for psychopathy. This analysis was not justified in their Introduction, but it is interesting to know. They do not mention if this pattern concurs with prior research.

Paired-sample *t*-tests require interval or ratio data, the data should come from a normal distribution and there should be homogeneity of variance. The distribution of scores on the dark trial variables were each reported as being 'close to' normal (2018, p. 3). The reported standard deviations were of comparable size, so homogeneity of variance can be assumed. As the 5-point scales of the SDT are often considered to produce interval data (see GQ2), these tests are appropriate. If the data are, instead, considered ordinal, then the Wilcoxon matched-pairs signed ranks test, or the sign test, should have been used instead.

SEM is a standard multivariate technique that is used when researchers have an *a priori* model of causal relationships between latent variables, as such, it is appropriate. Kowalski *et al.* constructed a model to examine whether the latent variables Machiavellianism, psychopathy and narcissism are predicted by the latent variable fluid intelligence, as measured by Raven's SPM, while controlling for error associated with the measurement of each variable (see Figure 4.1).

There is some debate whether individual items from questionnaires should be used in SEM (here, the 27 questions from the SDT, nine for each dark triad trait), or whether they can be allocated into a smaller number of 'parcels' to simplify the model and its interpretation (Little *et al.*, 2005). Kowalski *et al.* chose to create three parcels for the Machiavellian, psychopath and narcissism SDT subscales separately, making nine parcels in total. They used an item-to-construct balance approach to construct their parcels, which should produce parcels for each personality trait that are balanced in terms or item difficulty and item discrimination.

With this approach, the association each SDT item has with Raven's SPM score is calculated. Then, for each subscale of the SDT, the first three items with the highest associations, or loadings, are assigned to parcels 1, 2 and 3 in that order. The next three highest loading items are then assigned to the parcels in the reverse order, so that the fourth highest loading item would be allocated to parcel 3, the fifth highest loading item to parcel 2 and the sixth highest loading item to parcel 1. This sequence continues until all items have been allocated, so the seventh highest loading item would be allocated to parcel 1, the eighth to parcel 2 and the ninth to parcel 3. This to-and-fro order of allocation of items to parcels aims to ensure item difficulty is balanced within the parcels for each dark triad, but it is not necessarily matched between the dark triads.

It would have been interesting to have seen which items ended up with which others in each parcel, but we are not told.

To conduct SEM, there should be a reasonably large sample size, multivariate normality, interval or ratio data and, for Kowalski *et al.*, a linear relationship between the variables. The sample size, 128, with nine observed variables from the SDT in the model, yields a ratio of nearly 13 to 1, which is reasonable (10 to 1 is generally considered acceptable). As previously mentioned, the 5-point Likert scales used in the SDT can be construed as interval data, and the data from Raven's SPM are ratio. The data from Raven's SPM were not normally distributed, however, but they did not attempt to correct for this (for an introduction to possible data transformations, see Osborne, 2003). The data also did not meet the multivariate normality criterion (Mardia's test). Kowalski *et al.* report that because of this, they used the robust maximum likelihood estimation (MLE) method. They do not, however, mention whether they made the adjustments necessary when using MLE with non-normal data (Hayashi, Bentler & Yuan, 2011). The SEM approach is appropriate for the research questions they wanted to ask, with the caveat that not all of the requirements for SEM with MLE may have been met.

The authors provide a histogram of the residual errors for intelligence scores. The distribution is negatively skewed – many of the error terms cluster around slightly positive values – and there are two low-scoring outliers; nevertheless, Kowalski *et al.* consider the residual errors not to differ substantially from a normal distribution with a mean of zero.

Kowalski *et al.* had three concerns about their SEM: first, the two participants who had outlying intelligence scores; second, their students had slightly higher intelligence scores than the norms for the Polish population; third, their SEM explained little of the variance in the intelligence scores. This is why they created two subgroups for fluid intelligence: the third of participants with the lowest Raven's SPM scores, and the third with the highest (see GQ5). They then compared these low and high intelligence groups on their Machiavellian, psychopathy and narcissism scores with three independent-samples *t*-tests and performed three correlations on the same data, presumably Pearson's *r*.

7. What was the main result?
7.1. The structural equation model (SEM)
The SEM fit parameters all indicated that their model was a good fit to their data: χ^2 $p > 0.05$; comparative fit index, CFI = 0.97; standardised root mean square residual, SRMR = 0.05 (Parry, 2020).[3] The residual errors from modelling the intelligence scores were approximately normally distributed, with a mean of zero. The standardised regression coefficients, *b*, indicated that only Machiavellianism was significantly predicted by scores on Raven's SPM (*b* = 0.31).

The latent variables representing the dark triad traits (the ovals in Figure 4.1) were significantly intercorrelated (*r* = 0.72 for Machiavellianism and psychopathy, *r* = 0.54 for Machiavellianism and narcissism and

Figure 4.1 The structural equation model (SEM) set up by Kowalski *et al.* In SEM notation, measured or observed variables are indicated by boxes, latent variables by ovals. Single-headed arrows from latent variables to measured variables (the parcels) are equivalent to factor loadings. Double-headed arrows between the latent variables indicate the correlations between them. The latent variable fluid intelligence is also represented by a box, but its position in the hierarchy shows that Kowalski *et al.* assume it causes variation in the latent variables. The single-headed arrows from the fluid intelligence box to the latent variables represent hypothetical causal relationships, signified by b, the standardised regression coefficient. Only the association between fluid intelligence and Machiavellianism was statistically significant ($b = 0.31$). Asterisks denote significant associations. M = Machiavellian, N = narcissism, P = psychopathy; 1–9 are the items from the M, N and P subscales of the SDT questionnaire, ranked in order of their association with Raven's SPM scores. They were allocated in this way to balance item difficulty and discriminability within each set of three parcels.

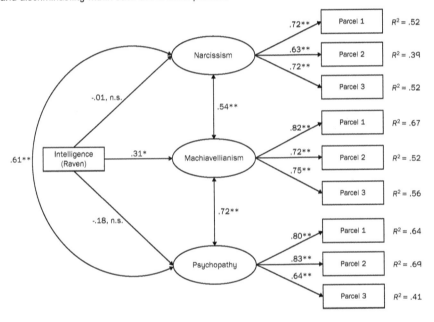

$r = 0.61$ for psychopathy and narcissism). The factor loadings between each of the dark triad latent variables and their three parcels of intelligence were all greater than 0.6, and were statistically significant, indicating that aspects of each dark triad latent variable were well captured by the SDT questionnaire items.

Recap: The χ^2 statistic can be used as a test of association or a test of the goodness of fit of data to an expected outcome or model. Here it is used as a test of goodness of fit to the SEM. In this context, however, it is better called a test of badness of fit, as it indicates a good model fit only if it is not significant.

7.2. The raw data: dark triad personalities and intelligence

Kowalski *et al.* provide a site to download their data, so direct correlations between the Raven SPM scores and the ratings of each dark triad trait can be calculated and compared graphically. These are shown in the scatterplots in Figure 4.2. The clouds of points in each chart clearly do not show a strong relationship between the SPM scores and any of the

Figure 4.2 Scatterplots showing the correlations between Raven's SPM and Machiavellianism, psychopathy and narcissism.

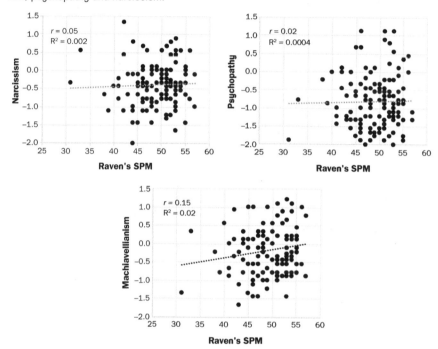

dark triad ratings, however, the correlation between Raven's SPM and Machiavellianism was statistically significant, paralleling the results from the SEM ($r = 0.15, p = 0.04$, one-tailed test: the correlation was in the predicted direction).[4]

Kowalski *et al.* then took the highest third of intelligence scores and the lowest third and performed three independent-samples *t*-tests, one for each dark triad. The only significant result was for Machiavellianism: the high intelligence group scored significantly higher on Machiavellianism than the low intelligence group, and there was again a significant positive association between Machiavellian ratings and intelligence scores (this again was presumably Pearson's correlation coefficient, $r = 0.19$) (Figure 4.3). This correlation is again only significant with a one-tailed test ($p = 0.04$, two-tailed $p = 0.08$).

Figure 4.3 Scatterplots showing the correlations between Raven's SPM and Machiavellianism, psychopathy and narcissism for those participants whose SPM scores lay in the top and bottom thirds of the range of scores.

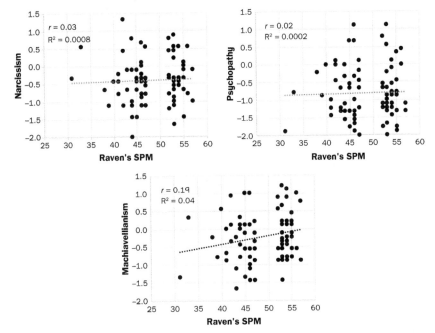

It is not entirely clear what these correlations are supposed to achieve. After finding a significant group difference between those in the low and high intelligence groups and their Machiavellianism ratings, it is inevitable that the correlation between intelligence and Machiavellianism ratings will be significant. Kowalski et al. also correct the correlations for a restriction in the range of scores (without saying what the correction was), however, the range of scores in the full data set, and in the data from only those participants with the highest and lowest scores, is the same. The range is the maximum score minus the minimum score and, by selecting the highest and lowest thirds from the range of scores, the maximum and minimum will necessarily be the same in both data sets.

7.3. The raw data: intercorrelations between Machiavellianism, psychopathy and narcissism

Kowalski *et al.* first report that the three dark triad personalities from the SDT questionnaire were highly intercorrelated but do not present any correlation coefficients, nor do they present these intercorrelations graphically. Since their data are available on-line, the relevant scatterplots and correlation coefficients are presented in Figure 4.4. All were statistically significant ($p < 0.001$). The data have been re-coded on a scale from –2 to +2 rather than from 1 ('strongly disagree') to 5 ('strongly agree'). With the re-coded scale, 0 represents neither agree nor disagree, values less than zero denote people who do not endorse Machiavellian, narcissistic or psychopathic statements, and values above zero denote people who do. The shaded regions show the data for people who do not endorse Machiavellian, narcissistic or psychopathic statements. It is instructive to look at these figures and consider what is driving the intercorrelations.

If you just take the data from those students who do endorse at least one of the Machiavellian, narcissistic or psychopathic traits and remove all those who endorsed none of them, 59 students remain and the pattern of results is very different: only the correlation between Machiavellianism and psychopathy remains statistically significant at $p < 0.05$ (Figure 4.5). So what drove the correlations with all of the data: that not being a narcissist is associated with not being a psychopath or Machiavellian rather than being a narcissist is associated with being a psychopath whether or not you are a Machiavellian?

Figure 4.4 Scatterplots showing the correlations between Machiavellianism, psychopathy and narcissism.

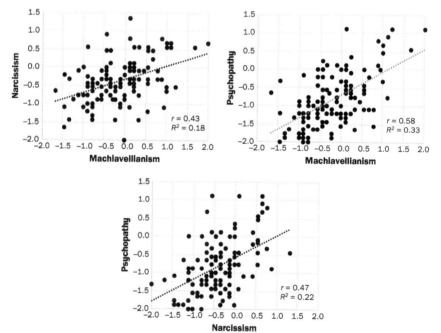

Figure 4.5 Scatterplots showing the correlations between Machiavellianism, psychopathy and narcissism when only those students who endorsed experiencing at least one of these traits are retained.

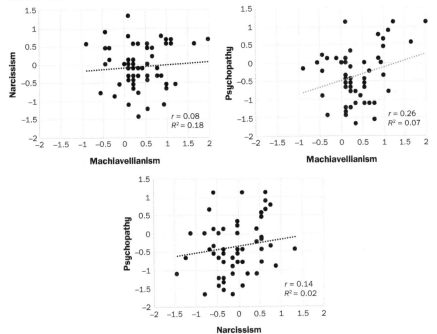

8. What conclusions were drawn? Were they valid? Kowalski *et al.* concluded that Machiavellianism is associated with better performance on Raven's SPM, compared with narcissism or psychopathy. This conclusion is justified from their study and the SEM analysis performed. They justifiably comment on limitations in their study, such as testing high school students with a limited age range and having a greater number of females than males.

9. What are your main criticisms of the report?
Major limitations include:

1 The sample tested (high school students, limited age range, gender bias: the majority were female). This impacts the external validity of the study, as the results are not readily generalisable to a wider population.

2 The items of the SDT questionnaire, some of which may not be relevant to teenagers. This impacts the external validity of their study

3 The testing situation: simultaneously testing many students in a classroom, some of whom finished Raven's SPM earlier than others by half an hour. This impacts the internal validity of the study

4   They do not mention what other questionnaires were administered, and in what order.

5   Who administered the questionnaires and Raven's SPM, and were they known to the students? This could affect the way the students respond: if the administrator is a teacher or school psychologist, known to the students, the students may be inclined to either exaggerate or curtail their responses to the questionnaires

6   There is little discussion of their results in the Discussion section; the authors focus more on prior literature rather than interrogating their own results

7   There is no discussion about dark triad traits and age or gender in previously published research.

10. What are the main strengths of the report? Kowalski *et al.* made a clear case for contrasting crystallised and fluid intelligence, emphasising that previous studies have assessed crystallised intelligence only. To the extent that Raven's SPM addresses fluid intelligence in 16–18-year-olds, this was a valid extension of previous research into intelligence and the dark triad.

Exercises

1   What predictions do the authors make about intelligence, Machiavellianism, narcissism and psychopathy? Does the cited literature justify their predictions? Comment on the method and the sample selected and the implications these may have on the conclusions that are able to be drawn.

2   Were the analyses clearly presented and driven by any hypotheses? Which statistical tests were used? What was the main conclusion and was it justified?

> **Rauthmann, J. F., & Kolar, G. P. (2013). The perceived attractiveness and traits of the Dark Triad: Narcissists are perceived as hot, Machiavellians and psychopaths not. *Personality and Individual Differences*, 54(5), 582–586. https://doi.org/10.1016/j.paid.2012.11.005.**

As mentioned in the Introduction to this chapter, people with dark triad personalities are sometimes portrayed as people we like to dislike, but are they sometimes likeable? Rauthmann and Kolar (2013) pick up on the idea that they can appear attractive, at least initially, until you get to know them better and the darker side of their personalities seeps out. Because they focus on themselves and on advancing their own interests, dark triad personalities can appear successful in life and at work, which some people find appealing. Rauthmann and Kolar wanted to examine whether the dark triad personalities are equally attractive to other people, or whether one is more likeable than the others.

Synopsis

Introduction

Rauthmann and Kolar (2013) begin with the observation that, as a consequence of their tendency to manipulate people around them for their own gain, dark triad personalities often 'get ahead' at the expense of 'getting along' with other people. As their tactics can make them successful socially or at work, they can initially appear appealing to those around them. The authors summarise the characteristics of each, describing Machiavellians as cynical, callous and manipulative; psychopaths as cold, manipulative and impulsive; and narcissists as attention-seeking, vain and arrogant. They cite previous research that has drawn similarities between the three, including success at short-term relationships despite low agreeableness. As with the review by Kowalski *et al.*, Rauthmann and Kolar raise the debate whether the dark triad personalities are nuances of one underlying dark core, or whether they are differentiable. They wish to see how lay people judge these personalities: do they discriminate between them, or are they perceived as similar? The issue raised, therefore, does not assess whether the dark personalities actually differ, or whether they overlap, but whether other people perceive them as differing. They comment that there are few studies on how these three are perceived (indeed, a literature search on 'how are dark triad personalities perceived' brought up few references prior to 2013, other than by the authors). They suggest previous work has examined the perception of the dark triad personalities separately, not all in the one study.

Rauthmann and Kolar state that 'there are probably differences in how narcissists, Machiavellians and psychopaths are judged although interpersonal perception studies on the full Dark Triad (not only one member) are scarce' (2013, p. 583). In the present study, however, they recruit a large number of participants and then divide them into three groups: one group judges a narcissist, a separate group judges a Machiavellian and a third judges a psychopath. By running a between-groups study, their criticism applies to themselves as well.

Their first hypothesis, which they say is based on the literature outlined previously, is that narcissists would be perceived the most favourably of the three (more agreeable and conscientious), whereas Machiavellians and psychopaths would be perceived to be similar or identical.

They cite one of their earlier studies (Rauthmann & Kolar, 2012) where they had investigated how Machiavellians, psychopaths and narcissists are perceived when participants simply read descriptions of each, and found that narcissists were judged more favourably than Machiavellians and psychopaths, who were judged to be similarly unfavourable. In this paper, Rauthmann and Kolar wish to assess how individuals judge *people* with dark traits, rather than judging the traits when presented as a series of statements that were read without a context.

The organisation of details could be improved in the Introduction. For example, nowhere in the preceding part of their Introduction is there anything that would differentiate Machiavellians from psychopaths or narcissists. In the subsequent paragraph they cite literature that could perhaps substantiate this hypothesis. There they cite studies that have shown narcissists to be popular and attractive, to have high status, and to be successful at short-term relationships, making them desirable as friends or partners. Earlier, Rauthmann and Kolar had attributed success at short-term relationships to Machiavellians and psychopaths as well, yet now they say Machiavellians and psychopaths should appear undesirable as friends or partners. The Introduction is also somewhat repetitive.

Methods

Rauthmann and Kolar asked a group of undergraduate seminar students to each test 10 people not associated with a university. Each had to test five women and five men. They collected usable data from 184 participants, 95 females and 89 males, which were divided into three groups. They presented their participants with information on a fictitious opposite-sex person. Each group received information on a person who scored highly on narcissism ($N = 60$), Machiavellianism ($N = 64$) or psychopathy ($N = 60$) scales. The scales came from the Dirty Dozen (Jonason & Webster, 2010) and comprise four statements each:

- **Narcissism:** I tend to (i) want others to admire me; (ii) want others to pay attention to me; (iii) expect special favours from others; (iv) seek prestige or status.
- **Machiavellianism:** I have (i) used deceit or lied to get my own way; (ii) used flattery to get my own way. I tend to (iii) manipulate others to get my own way; (iv) exploit others towards my own end.
- **Psychopathy:** I tend to (i) lack remorse; (ii) be callous or insensitive; (iii) not to be too concerned with morality or the morality of my actions; (iv) be cynical.

It would have been useful if Rauthmann and Kolar had presented all four questions for each scale, so that the reader could judge for themselves how sensible their procedure was. All they did present was one example from each scale. They also did not specifically say how these fictitious characters were presented to their participants: were the Dirty Dozen statements just read, or were they woven into a story of some sort? The way this information was relayed to the participants is crucial to be able to judge how sensible this study is. Rauthmann and Kolar simply refer to 'vignettes'. In the Discussion, however, they state that their participants read these statements exactly, but they do not say if they were bluntly given, or incorporated into some sort of narrative. Rauthmann and Kolar refer to these fictitious characters in the plural throughout the Results section and mention that the fictitious people scored highly (3 or 4) on each of the Dirty Dozen scales, which implies there were indeed multiple stories made up to incorporate each trait, rather than simply reading out the Dirty Dozen statements and suggesting they describe a person. An example vignette would have been helpful to understand what was actually done. The lack of detail undermines both the internal and external validity of the study.

The participants had to rate the fictitious person's likeability, friend value, attractiveness, short-term mate value and long-term mate value. They also completed the Big Five (15 questions) and Agency/Communion (20 questions). All were rated on 5-point scales where 0 = 'not at all' and 4 = 'totally'. These endpoints are not appropriate for the personality ratings. The Dirty Dozen should be scored using 5-point scales with endpoints 'strongly disagree' and 'strongly agree' (Jonason & Webster, 2010), the Agency and Communion scales should be scored using 7-point scales with endpoints 'not at all' and 'very much' (Gebauer, Paulhus & Neberich, 2013), and the Big Five should be assessed with 5-point scales with categories 'strongly disagree', 'disagree', 'neither agree nor disagree', 'agree', 'strongly agree' (John & Srivastava, 1999). Rauthmann and Kolar do not explain why they have chosen to use their own rating scales for the personality ratings rather than those that should be used; presumably they wanted to have the same scales for each variable, but that is no justification. What they have done compromises the validity of the data collected. Furthermore, scales with endpoints 'not at all' and 'totally' generate ordinal, not interval, data.

Rauthmann and Kolar do not say what the Big Five are: they are extraversion, agreeableness, openness to experience, conscientiousness and neuroticism. They give citations, but a brief description of each and what they cover would have been useful in the text. They are listed in a table, but not identified. There is no definition of agency or of communion.

Results

Rauthmann and Kolar conducted a multivariate analysis of variance (MANOVA) using seven dependent variables (the ratings on the Big Five and Agency and Communion scales) and one between-subjects factor (whether the fictitious character was a Machiavellian, psychopath or narcissist). They report a significant overall effect of condition (group: what type of fictitious character was being rated). They refine this significant effect with seven one-way analyses of variance (ANOVA) and report that group only affected the ratings of neuroticism, extraversion, agreeableness, conscientiousness and communion. They followed these analyses with multiple (21) pairwise post-hoc comparisons, with Bonferroni correction. The narcissist was judged more favourably than the Machiavellian or psychopath on agreeableness and communality, and was judged as more extraverted than the psychopath and more conscientious than the Machiavellian. He/she was, however, also judged to be more neurotic than the Machiavellian or the psychopath. The Machiavellian and the psychopath were judged to be quite similar except that the Machiavellian was judged to be more neurotic than the psychopath.

> *Rauthmann and Kolar refer to the pairwise comparisons as post-hoc, but they would be more accurately described as a priori since they are comparing the Machiavellian, psychopathic and narcissistic vignettes on each of the personality variables, which were planned comparisons from the start of the study. These were presumably independent-samples t-tests, but this is not explicitly stated.*

Rauthmann and Kolar conducted a second MANOVA on the attractiveness ratings using five dependent variables and the same between-subjects factor of condition/group. They report again a significant overall effect of group (what type of personality was being rated). They followed this overall effect with five one-way ANOVAs: group had an effect on all five attractiveness ratings. Rauthmann and Kolar just report a 'general pattern' following multiple (15) pairwise comparisons: the narcissist was perceived the most favourably, while the Machiavellian and psychopath were judged to be similar. They do not say if this was true for all of the attractiveness ratings, they just refer to a general pattern. Looking at their table of descriptive statistics (see Table 4.1 in GQ7), it is clear that the narcissist was perceived as more attractive on all five attractiveness variables. It also appears, however, that the psychopath was perceived as more likeable and more likely to be wanted as a friend than the Machiavellian, whereas the Machiavellian was perceived as more attractive and more likely to be wanted as a short-term partner than the psychopath. Without further details, it is impossible to tell which differences were statistically significantly different.

Conclusions

Rauthmann and Kolar conclude that their hypotheses were largely supported: while none of the fictional personalities were perceived as particularly appealing, the narcissist was judged more favourably than the Machiavellian or the psychopath. The authors end with speculation on why this may be the case. They also raise a comment at the end on their use of the Dirty Dozen because its validity has been questioned, even at the time Rauthmann and Kolar were completing their study (Miller *et al.*, 2012) and it has since been more widely criticised as not adequately differentiating between the dark triad personalities (e.g. Maples, Lamkin & Miller, 2014; Carter *et al.*, 2015).[5]

The ten general questions (10GQs)

When this article has been discussed in class, stumbling blocks have included the assumptions required to perform parametric tests (correlation, analysis of variance, multivariate analysis of variance) and the perennial issue of the level of measurement when rating scales are used.

1(a). Does the report specify an hypothesis? If so, what is it? Is there more than one? Rauthmann and Kolar have three clear hypotheses regarding personality measures: (i) that narcissists will be perceived more favourably on personality measures than Machiavellians; (ii) that narcissists will be perceived more favourably on the same personality measures than psychopaths; (iii) that Machiavellians and psychopaths will be perceived similarly or virtually identically. The first two are directional, the third predicts a null hypothesis. In fact, they assessed seven measures of personality, so that equates to 14 directional hypotheses and seven predictions of a null hypothesis.

As has been mentioned when discussing Kowalski et al. (2018), it is never a good idea to predict a null hypothesis: see discussion of GQ1 for the paper by Kowalski et al. earlier in this chapter. It is certainly not a good idea to predict multiple null hypotheses.

1(b). What background or rationale is provided as justification for any hypothesis? Rauthmann and Kolar comment that there are few studies that have looked at how all three members of the dark triad are perceived in one study rather than individually. They mention one of their own studies that had assessed self-ratings and ratings of others in a naturalistic setting. Minimally acquainted students worked in pairs on a task requiring cooperation, they then rated themselves and rated their partner on the Big Five, intelligence and dark triad characteristics (Rauthmann, 2012). There it was reported that Machiavellians diverged from narcissists and psychopaths on all types of ratings, whereas narcissists' and psychopaths' ratings were similar.

They refer to another one of their own studies as justification for their hypotheses (Rauthmann & Kolar, 2012). In that study, their participants had rated the desirability and advantageousness (for themselves and for others) of other people when they exhibited traits from the Dirty Dozen, and of themselves when they acted in a similar way. Importantly, the statements describing aspects of each trait were rated individually, out of context. This time they found that narcissists were judged more favourably than Machiavellians and psychopaths were judged to be more similar. In the present study, they wish to extend this latter work by asking their participants to judge fictitious *people* who exhibit the Dirty Dozen characteristics, rather than judge statements in isolation. If this is a sensible approach, their study is an extension of previous research from this group.

The results from Rauthmann (2012) differ from the results from Rauthmann and Kolar (2012) and the predictions made for Rauthmann and Kolar (2013). Rauthmann and Kolar (2013) comment that Rauthmann (2012) compared peer-reports and self-views in a naturalistic setting. Rauthmann and Kolar (2012) presented statements associated with each dark trait in isolation. That may be the explanation for the different pattern of results in the two studies. It is plausible that, in Rauthmann (2012), the participants were simultaneously rating another person and themselves on all three dimensions of the dark triad, together, and overlap across the triad traits could come into play. In Rauthmann and Kolar (2012), and in the present study, they are examining dark personalities in isolation: they cannot assess any overlap between them. They are deliberately looking at each trait in isolation, since, not only do they state that 'there are probably differences in how narcissists, Machiavellians and psychopaths are judged although interpersonal perception studies on the full Dark Triad (not only one member) are scarce', but go on to add, 'This makes it difficult to examine unique personality profiles of narcissists, Machiavellians and psychopaths' (2013, p. 583). Is it valid to create a fictional 'pure' or 'unique' narcissist, Machiavellian or psychopath, when they cite literature showing they share several traits as well? They want to 'elucidate more stringently and systematically how they [the dark triad personalities] are perceived in appeal and personality traits' (ibid.). Nowhere in the cited literature is there the suggestion that the dark triad personalities present a 'unique' personality profile and that assessing them in isolation would provide a more stringent or systematic elucidation of any aspect of them.

2(a). Specify all the variables in the investigation and indicate what sort of variables they are (e.g. dependent vs. independent, manipulated, controlled, nuisance, confounding). Specify what level of measurement has been achieved for each dependent

variable (nominal, ordinal, interval, ratio). There is one independent variable: dark triad group, as participants were allocated into three groups according to what sort of fictitious character they were asked to rate (Machiavellian, psychopath or narcissist).

There were 12 dependent variables in total: five personality styles from the Big Five – neuroticism, extraversion, openness, agreeableness and conscientiousness, together with agency and communion; and five attractiveness items – likeability, preference as a platonic friend, attractiveness, preference for a short-term relationship and preference for a long-term relationship. All were rated on 5-point rating scales where 0 denoted 'not at all' and 4 denoted 'totally'. The authors do not say whether scale points 1, 2 and 3 were labelled or were left to be interpreted by each individual participant. These are ordinal scales but they are treated as if they are interval for the analyses.

Gender is a controlled variable, as there were approximately equal numbers of males and females.

There were multiple testers (undergraduates from a seminar class who each approached ten people to participate). How the fictitious characters were allocated to each student is not made explicit. If one student only had, for example, Machiavellian characters and another had only psychopaths, or only narcissists, then the tester would be a nuisance variable. Ideally, each tester would have been given a mixture of the three personality types. In addition, Rauthmann and Kolar do not comment on how, or if, they standardised the test procedure across the multiple testers. Some sort of training should have been given to the students so that there was a uniform presentation of the vignettes. Another nuisance associated with the testers is whether they were known to the participants. Imagine yourself in the experiment and a friend comes up to you, asks you to read a description of a possibly unpleasant character, and then asks you if you would like to have a short- or long-term relationship with that character, might you feel embarrassed if you said 'yes'?

Rauthmann and Kolar did not assess their participants for dark triad traits. This is another nuisance variable because, with 184 participants, it is likely that some of them exhibited Machiavellian, psychopathic or narcissistic traits. For example, if any of their participants had Machiavellian tendencies and were asked to rate either another Machiavellian character, or one of the others, their own predisposition may affect how they respond. Would they like to have another Machiavellian as a friend or partner, or would they feel threatened? The same applies if any of their participants exhibited psychopathy or narcissism, or any combination of the three.

Boredom or fatigue could be another nuisance variable if the questionnaires were all administered in the same order. Every participant completed every questionnaire, so it is not a confound. The questionnaires should nevertheless have been completed in different orders by different participants to avoid boredom or fatigue.

Test location could be another nuisance variable as we are not told when and where the participants were tested. Responses may differ if the participants were at home, in a café, in a laboratory, in a classroom, in a park. Uncontrolled, distracting events could be happening around them and affected their concentration and responses.

Another nuisance variable is the sexual preference of the participants. Rauthmann and Kolar emphasise that each participant judged a fictitious character of the opposite sex but, when it comes to relationships, not everyone prefers a relationship with someone of the opposite sex. There is no indication they asked their participants about their sexual preference (and there would have been some ethical questions raised if they did regarding disclosure of personal information to a student). They could have asked their participants to read the vignettes and imagine the vignette was describing a person of their preferred sexual orientation to get around having to ask their participants directly. Do you think that would be an appropriate solution?

2(b). Do the selected variables address the research hypothesis/ hypotheses? Raven's SPM is a standard test that is routinely used to assess at least one aspect of non-verbal, fluid intelligence and thereby does address the hypotheses regarding fluid intelligence.

The SDT is an established questionnaire, with over 1,100 citations in 2020. It comprises 27 questions divided between three sub-scales, one for each of the dark triad personalities. Kowalski *et al.* quote reliability coefficients for their sample that are greater than 0.7 for each subscale (Cronbach's a: 0.71 for narcissism and 0.78 for both Machiavellianism and psychopathy[2]). This questionnaire is appropriate as a way to assess Machiavellianism, narcissism and psychopathy, although it has been criticised for not adequately differentiating between Machiavellianism and psychopathy (Persson, Kajonius and Garcia, 2019). See (Furnham *et al.*, 2014) for a review of alternative questionnaires.

One issue with the SDT, however, is its appropriateness for use with mostly 16 year olds. Items on the psychopathy scale include, for example, *I enjoy having sex with people I hardly know and I have never gotten into trouble with the law* (these are reverse coded when it comes to combining the scales, so strongly agree becomes strongly disagree and so on for the five scale categories). These questions may be a little early for some of their students. A second issue is who administered it: if the questionnaires were handed out by the students' teachers, that may have influenced how truthful their responses would be. They may be concerned that they could be identified, or they may think it amusing to depict a maverick personality, perhaps to see the effect it had on their teacher when later they were (presumably) de-briefed. They may tend to brag or boast so they can show off with their peers later on, rather than respond truthfully. Sixteen and 17 are peculiar ages and different students are at different stages of maturity.

3. What did the participants have to do? (briefly) Is the study easily replicable? Participants were approached by undergraduate students and were presumably friends or family. The undergraduates were tasked with testing ten people each, five women and five men. The only detail we are given about the participants is their average age ± one standard deviation (23.8 years ± 5.8 years), age range (17–54 years), the gender divide (95 females and 89 males) and that they were not themselves university students.[6] There is no mention of ethics, consent, or of debriefing at the end of the session.

The participants were asked to read a description of a fictitious person who scored highly on Machiavellianism, psychopathy or narcissism. It is not clear what the participants actually had to read: in their Discussion, Rauthmann and Kolar state that they read exactly the items from the Dirty Dozen. They also refer to fictitious Machiavellians, psychopaths and narcissists in the plural, so presumably several fictitious characters were created and the Dirty Dozen items were woven into narratives of some sort.

Having read the description of a fictitious, opposite-sex person, the participants were asked to rate them on the Big Five, on agency and communion and on attractiveness.

The study is not replicable, as we do not know what the participants read about each fictitious character, and we do not know how these fictitious people were allocated to the undergraduate students. Rauthmann and Kolar provide no details about when and where their participants were tested.

4(a). What experimental design was used? This is a mixed experimental design if we assume the participants were randomly allocated to the three groups. There is one between-subjects variable: group (whether the person was allocated to read a description of a Machiavellian, a psychopath or a narcissist). There are 12 within-subjects variables (the five scales from the Big Five, agency and communion and the five attractiveness ratings).

4(b). Do the method and design address the research hypothesis/ hypotheses? In principle, the method and design could address the research hypotheses but, in practice, it is impossible to tell due to the lack of information on the actual test materials used (the descriptions of each of the dark triad personalities) and the test procedure.

5. What comparisons were chosen for statistical analysis? Rauthmann and Kolar first looked at associations between each of the seven personality ratings, and between each of the five attractiveness ratings, before comparing the ratings between the three groups (Machiavellianism, psychopathy and narcissism).

6. What analysis was used? Was it appropriate? Associations between the personality ratings, and between the attractiveness ratings, were assessed with correlation (presumably Pearson's correlation coefficient). These were followed by two one-way multivariate analyses of variance (MANOVA), one for the personality ratings, and one for the attractiveness ratings. Overall significant effects of group were further explored with multiple one-way analyses of variance (ANOVA) and post-hoc pairwise comparisons, presumably independent-samples t-tests, although this is not stated.

MANOVA and ANOVA are parametric tests and assume a reasonable sample size, interval or ratio data, a normal distribution of each dependent variable, homogeneity of variance, a linear relationship between the dependent variables and no multicollinearity: the dependent variables should be only moderately intercorrelated. The data from all 12 rating scales are ordinal, yet they are being treated as interval, so the analyses are not appropriate. It is not uncommon, however, to treat data from the Big Five as interval, but it is not ideal. An overall score for each group was calculated for the 12 personality and five attractiveness dependent variables (see Table 4.1 in GQ7).

It only takes a little thought to appreciate the absurdity of calculating an average for 5-point scales with endpoints 'not at all' and 'totally'. What would that average tell you?

Some standard deviations are similar in size to their associated means, which indicates that those means are not a good summary of the data on which they are based. It would have been useful to see the mode for each dependent variable, as it is appropriate for ordinal data and shows what most people thought for each set of ratings.

The first step in conducting a MANOVA is to correlate the dependent variables: they should be moderate, neither too small nor too large. Rauthmann and Kolar do not present all of their correlations, just their range, which is from |0.01| to 0.52 for the analyses on the personality ratings. The absolute value of 0.01 is so small it is inconsequential, and they do not say which pair of variables produced that value, nor do they say if any other variables correlated so negligibly. There may be a clue which variables were involved in the outcome of the analyses – see GQ7. To conclude, the first MANOVA is problematic. It would have been more helpful to have presented all the correlation coefficients and then the reader could decide if a MANOVA with fewer dependent variables would have been more appropriate. The second MANOVA is appropriate, as the correlations between variables ranged from 0.29 to 0.66, with the caveat that the rating scales produce ordinal data.

Rauthmann and Kolar followed each MANOVA with multiple one-way ANOVAs (seven for the personality ratings and five for the attractiveness ratings) and then performed multiple pairwise comparisons. They could have compared their results to non-parametric alternatives such as multiple Kruskal-Wallis one-way analyses of variance followed by pairwise Mann-Whitney U-tests.

7. What was the main result? Rauthmann and Kolar first present means and standard deviations for each dependent variable (Table 4.1).

From the first MANOVA on personality ratings, Rauthmann and Kolar found that there was a significant main effect of group. The effect size (partial h^2) of 0.24 was large (Cohen, 1988).[7] This overall effect was examined with seven one-way ANOVAs, one for each of the seven personality variables. The three groups differed significantly for ratings of neuroticism, extraversion, agreeableness, conscientiousness and communion. Rauthmann and Kolar do not provide individual results for each of these analyses, they just report that F values ranged from 3.63 to 44.48, significance values (p) were all ≤ 0.028, and effect sizes (partial h^2) ranged from 0.04 to 0.33.

As openness and agency did not differ significantly between the groups, it may be that these were the variables that correlated so negligibly with one of the other dependent variables or with each other.

These analyses were followed with multiple pairwise comparisons, with Bonferroni correction. Rauthmann and Kolar provide no details of the results of these tests, or what sort of tests were used (presumably independent-samples t-tests), just the overall outcome. The narcissist character was more agreeable and communal than the Machiavellian or psychopath, he/she was more extraverted than the psychopath and more conscientious than the Machiavellian. He/she was, however, judged to be more neurotic than either the Machiavellian or the psychopath. The Machiavellian and psychopath characters were perceived fairly similarly, except that the Machiavellian character was perceived as more neurotic than the psychopath.

The second MANOVA on attractiveness ratings also produced a significant main effect of group, with a reasonably large effect size (partial h^2) of 0.13. Rauthmann and Kolar conducted one-way ANOVA on each of the five attractiveness ratings. Group differed significantly for all five. Again, they just report the range of F values (7.99–16.17), significant p (all < 0.001) and effect sizes (partial $h^2 = 0.08$–0.15). Multiple pairwise comparisons, again with Bonferroni correction, showed 'generally' that the narcissist was perceived as more attractive on all five measures, while the Machiavellian and psychopath were perceived similarly. As mentioned in the synopsis, however, their table of descriptive statistics shows that the psychopath was perceived as more likeable and more likely to be

Table 4.1 Means and standard deviations (SD) for the personality and attractiveness ratings of each fictitious character

	Machiavellian Mean ± SD	Psychopath Mean ± SD	Narcissist Mean ± SD
Personality ratings			
Neuroticism	1.3 ± 0.9	**0.8 ± 0.7**	2.3 ± 1.0
Extraversion	2.8 ± 0.8	2.5 ± 0.8	2.9 ± 0.7
Openness	1.8 ± 0.9	1.6 ± 0.7	1.8 ± 0.8
Agreeableness	1.2 ± 0.7	1.1 ± 0.7	1.5 ± 0.7
Conscientiousness	2.1 ± 0.8	2.2 ± 0.9	2.5 ± 0.7
Agency	2.6 ± 0.4	2.4 ± 0.5	2.6 ± 0.4
Communion	0.9 ± 0.6	**0.9 ± 0.7**	1.4 ± 0.7
Attractiveness ratings			
Likeability	**0.9 ± 0.7**	**1.2 ± 1.0**	1.8 ± 0.9
Friend	**0.8 ± 0.9**	**1.1 ± 1.2**	1.7 ± 1.0
Attractiveness	**1.3 ± 1.1**	1.0 ± 1.0	1.9 ± 1.0
Short-term relationship	2.1 ± 1.2	**1.5 ± 1.4**	2.4 ± 1.3
Long-term relationship	**0.4 ± 0.8**	**0.5 ± 1.0**	1.0 ± 1.0

Note: Bold italicised entries show those entries where the standard deviation is about the same size as the mean, or larger than the mean, indicating that the mean is not a good summary of the underlying data. Shaded entries show variables that appear to differ between Machiavellians and psychopaths, although these are not included in Rauthmann and Kolar's discussion of the 'general pattern' of results, instead they are described as being similar. Note all of the scales ranged from 0 to 4; for all of the entries, what does the size of the means and standard deviations tell you?

wanted as a friend than the Machiavellian, whereas the Machiavellian was perceived as more attractive and more likely to be wanted as a short-term partner than the psychopath (see Table 4.1).

In a footnote, the authors comment that adding gender as a second between-subjects variable in both MANOVAs or as a covariate in two MANCOVAs (multivariate analysis of covariance) did not change the pattern of results. They comment that gender did not have any meaningful effects. This is a little surprising, as dark triad effects have been reported to be more prevalent in males (Carter *et al.*, 2015), but Rauthmann and Kolar do not comment on this discrepancy with prior research. In addition, they had excluded 16 from the analyses for not specifying their gender. They could have included all the data in their final analyses if their preliminary analyses had shown gender to have no effect.

The presentation of all of their results is somewhat sparse.

8. What conclusions were drawn? Were they valid? Rauthmann and Kolar conclude that they have support for their hypotheses. While none of these fictitious characters were perceived as particularly pleasant, the narcissist was perceived more favourably than the Machiavellian or psychopathic characters.

> *Is scoring more highly on extraversion necessarily favourable? Is scoring more highly on neuroticism necessarily bad, when all the scores are fairly low to begin with?*

9. What are your main criticisms of the report?

There are many problems with this brief research article. Foremost amongst these are the lack of internal and external validity on multiple counts:

1 The authors did not check the status of their participants for dark triad traits. This compromises the internal and external validity of the study.

2 Having cited studies that have highlighted certain similarities between the dark triad personalities, it is inexplicable that the authors thought that creating characters who are apparently 'purely' Machiavellian, psychopathic or narcissistic would elucidate anything. Their character descriptors, presented in isolation rather than in the context of the other two dark triad traits, are highly artificial. Their results could be an artefact of creating not only fictitious but mythical personalities. This compromises the internal and external validity of the study.

3 Rauthmann and Kolar provide no explanation for substituting the appropriate rating scales for the personality ratings with their own 5-point rating scales with endpoints 'not at all' and 'totally'. This compromises the internal and external validity of the study.

4 There are no details of what the caricatures/vignettes were, or how many there were. Who made them up? This compromises the internal and external validity of the study.

5 There are scant details of the procedure. For example, there is no mention of training the testers so that their testing would be standardised; there are no details on whether the questionnaires were administered in the same order, where the testing was performed, who was tested, or whether the participants were known to the testers. This compromises the internal and external validity of the study.

6 The authors do not explain why a between-group design was used, with separate groups rating each personality type, when they had criticised other studies for assessing dark triad types separately/just one triad at a time. This compromises the internal and external validity of the study.

7 The use of parametric tests with clearly non-parametric data. Not only are the scales ordinal, but some of the standard deviations are also as large as the mean (Table 4.1), indicating the mean is not a good summary of the underlying data. The mode could have been presented as an appropriate measure for ordinal data, and non-parametric one-way analyses of variance followed by Mann-Whitney U-tests could have been performed instead. This compromises the internal validity of the study.

8 The use of the Dirty Dozen: it provides a rather simplistic assessment of the dark triad personalities and its validity has been criticised – the three measures correlate with each other and indeed some studies have suggested they can be seen to tap a dark personality continuum rather than differentiate between the three (Carter et al., 2015). Alternative tests were available at the time Rauthmann and Kolar were designing their study (see the footnote at the end of the synopsis). As these alternatives are longer than the Dirty Dozen, one speculation is that they chose the Dirty Dozen to use a questionnaire that itself is quick and dirty at the expense of gathering sensible data.

9 The title does not reflect what the study found: none of the fictitious characters were perceived to be particularly appealing. Rauthmann and Kolar clearly like the choice of words, as they end their paper repeating them. This style of language is informal and the content is inaccurate.

10. What are the main strengths of the report? A bane of many studies is the selection of participants: many authors test undergraduates who participate for course credit. This typically results in a lack of generalisability: the age range tends to be limited, there is often a preponderance of one gender, and university students in Psychology are not necessarily representative of any group other than university students in Psychology. Generally, they also differ, for example, in terms of their education and how much available time they have. Their motivation can sometimes be questioned if they are participating for course credit – they will get the credit however diligently (or thoughtlessly) they complete the tasks. There is also the risk that they may be familiar with some of the test materials. It is, therefore, a strength of this study that they recruited participants who were not at university, although Rauthmann and Kolar do not provide any details as to who they were, what their backgrounds were or how diverse the sample wase.

Exercises

1   What is the general research question that the authors' seek to address in their study? Do the authors provide adequate background to differentiate narcissism, Machiavellianism and psychopathy? What specific predictions do the authors make? Evaluate the methodology and experimental design and comment on their suitability to test the authors' predictions. Is a between-group study appropriate, given the authors' criticism of earlier studies that examined just one element of the dark triad?

2   Evaluate the analyses that were performed: how well do they map onto the authors' general research question? What conclusions were drawn? Were they valid, given the analyses performed? Comment on the differences between narcissism, Machiavellianism and psychopathy. Comment on their future research proposals and the possibility of disambiguating Machiavellianism from psychopathy.

Notes

1   Kowalski *et al.* provide a link to their data files on-line: if you download the data, you can see ages ranged from 16 to 18 years.

2   Cronbach's alpha is a measure of internal consistency between the scale items. It gives an indication of how closely related the items are within each of the three subscales of the SDT. The closer to 1 Cronbach's alpha is, the more the items in each subscale are intercorrelated and the more reliable the subscale is considered to be.

3   Parry (2020) lists fit indices for SEM as follows: $\chi^2 p$ should be > 0.05 (the null hypothesis is that the model fits perfectly), the CFI should be ≥ 0.90 and the SRMR should be < 0.08.

4   The correlations between latent variables following SEM are not the same as simple correlations on the raw data due to the transformations of the data that are part of SEM. For Rauthmann and Kolar's model, for example, particular questions from each of the dark triad subscales were divided amongst three parcels to create the latent variables of Machiavellianism, psychopathy and narcissism and it is these that are correlated in SEM. The trends for both sets of correlations should be similar, however, if the model adequately captures the constructs of each of the dark triad traits.

5   Alternative, and better received, tests include the MACH-IV for Machiavellianism (Christie & Geis, 1970), the Narcissistic Personality Inventory (NPI-16; Ames, Rose & Anderson, 2006) and the Self-report Psychopathy Scale (SRP; Paulhus, Neumann & Hare, 2009). All were available when Rauthmann and Kolar were designing their study.

6   Rauthmann and Kolar actually provide average age $\pm$ one standard deviation, and the age range, for the 201 participants who were originally recruited. Sixteen were excluded for not answering the question about their gender, but they do not provide updated details for the remaining 184.

7   Cohen reports a rule of thumb for ANOVA and one-way MANOVA that a small effect size (h^2) is 0.01, a medium effect size is 0.06 and a large effect size is 0.14.

References

Ames, D. R., Rose, P., & Anderson, C. P. (2006). The NPI-16 as a short measure of narcissism. *Journal of Research in Personality*, *40*(4), 440–450. https://doi.org/10.1016/j.jrp.2005.03.002.

Bollen, K. A., & Noble, M. D. (2011). Structural equation models and the quantification of behavior. *Proceedings of the National Academy of Sciences USA*, *108*(suppl. 3), 15639–15646. https://doi.org/10.1073/pnas.1010661108.

Carter, G. L., Campbell, A. C., Muncer, S. *et al.* (2015). A Mokken analysis of the Dark Triad 'Dirty Dozen': Sex and age differences in scale structures, and issues with individual items. *Personality and Individual Differences*, *83*, 185–191. https://doi.org/10.1016/j.paid.2015.04.012.

Christie, R., & Geis, F. L. (1970). *Studies in Machiavellianism*. New York: Academic Press.

Cohen, J. (1988). *Statistical Power Analysis for the Behavioral Sciences*, 2nd edn. New York: Routledge.

Crowne, D. P., & Marlowe, D. (1960). A new scale of social desirability independent of psychopathology. *Journal of Consulting Psychology*, *24*(4), 349–354. https://doi.org/10.1037/h0047358.

Furnham, A., Richards, S. C., Rangel, L. *et al.* (2014). Measuring malevolence: Quantitative issues surrounding the Dark Triad of personality. *Personality and Individual Differences*, *67*, 114–121. https://doi.org/10.1016/j.paid.2014.02.001.

Gebauer, J. E., Paulhus, D. L., & Neberich, W. (2013). Big Two personality and religiosity across cultures: Communals as religious conformists and agentics as religious contrarians. *Social Psychological and Personality Science*, *4*(1), 21–30. https://doi.org/10.1177/1948550612442553.

Harris, T. (1988). *The Silence of the Lambs*. New York: St. Martin's Press.

Hayashi, K., Bentler, P. M., & Yuan, K. H. (2011). Structural equation modeling, in C. R. Rao, J. P. Miller, and D. C. Rao (eds.) *Essential Statistical Methods for Medical Statistics*. Burlington, MA: Elsevier, pp. 202–234.

John, O. P., & Srivastava, S. (1999). The Big-Five trait taxonomy: History, measurement, and theoretical perspectives, in L. A. Pervin and O. P. John (eds.) *Handbook of Personality: Theory and Research*. New York: Guilford Press, pp. 102–138.

Jonason, P. K., & Webster, G. D. (2010). The Dirty Dozen: A concise measure of the dark triad. *Psychological Assessment*, *22*(2), 420–432. https://doi.org/10.1037/a0019265.

Jones, D. N., & Paulhus, D. L. (2014). Introducing the Short Dark Triad (SD3): A brief measure of dark personality traits. *Assessment*, *21*(1), 28–41. https://doi.org/10.1177/1073191113514105.

Klimstra, T. A., Jeronimus, B. F., Sijtsema, J. J. *et al.* (2020). The unfolding dark side: Age trends in dark personality features. *Journal of Research in Personality*, *85*, 103915. https://doi.org/10.1016/j.jrp.2020.103915.

Kowalski, C. M., Kwiatkowska, K., Kwiatkowska, M. M. *et al.* (2018). The Dark Triad traits and intelligence: Machiavellians are bright, and narcissists and psychopaths are ordinary. *Personality and Individual Differences*, *135*, 1–6. https://doi.org/10.1016/j.paid.2018.06.049.

Little, T. D., Cunningham, W. A., Shahar, G. *et al.* (2005). To parcel or not to parcel: Exploring the question, weighing the merits. *Structural Equation Modeling*, *9*(2), 151–173. https://doi.org/10.1207/S15328007SEM0902_1.

Maples, J. L., Lamkin, J., & Miller, J. D. (2014). A test of two brief measures of the dark triad: The Dirty Dozen and short dark triad. *Psychological Assessment*, *26*(1), 326–331. https://doi.org/10.1037/a0035084.

Miller, J. D., Few, L. R., Seibert, L. A. *et al.* (2012). An examination of the Dirty Dozen measure of psychopathy: A cautionary tale about the costs of brief measures. *Psychological Assessment, 24*(4), 1048–1053. https://doi.org/10.1037/a0028583.

Osborne, J. W. (2003). Notes on the use of data transformations. *Practical Assessment, Research and Evaluation, 8*(6), 2002–2003. https://doi.org/10.7275/4vng-5608.

Parry, S. (2020). *Fit Indices Commonly Reported for CFA and SEM.* https://www.cscu. cornell.edu/news/Handouts/SEM_fit.pdf (accessed 20 April 2021).

Patton, J. H., Stanford, M. S., & Barratt, E. S. (1995). Factor structure of the Barratt impulsiveness scale. *Journal of Clinical Psychology, 51*(6), 768–774. https://doi. org/10.1002/1097-4679(199511)51.

Paulhus, D. L., Neumann, C. S., & Hare, R. D. (2009). *Manual for the Self-report Psychopathy Scale.* Toronto: Multi-Health Systems.

Persson, B. N., Kajonius, P. J., & Garcia, D. (2019). Revisiting the structure of the Short Dark Triad. *Assessment, 26*(1), 3–16. https://doi.org/10.1177/1073191117701192.

Rauthmann, J. F. (2012). The Dark Triad and interpersonal perception: Similarities and differences in the social consequences of narcissism, Machiavellianism, and psychopathy. *Social Psychological and Personality Science, 3*(4), 487–496. https://doi. org/10.1177/1948550611427608.

Rauthmann, J. F., & Kolar, G. P. (2012). How 'dark' are the Dark Triad traits? Examining the perceived darkness of narcissism, Machiavellianism, and psychopathy. *Personality and Individual Differences, 53*(7), 884–889. https://doi.org/10.1016/j.paid. 2012.06.020.

Rauthmann, J. F., & Kolar, G. P. (2013). The perceived attractiveness and traits of the Dark Triad: Narcissists are perceived as hot, Machiavellians and psychopaths not. *Personality and Individual Differences, 54*(5), 582–586. https://doi.org/10.1016/j. paid.2012.11.005.

Raven, J. (1981). *Manual for Raven's Progressive Matrices and Vocabulary Scales. Research Supplement No. 1: The 1979 British Standardisation of the Standard Progressive Matrices and Mill Hill Vocabulary Scales, Together with Comparative Data from Earlier Studies in the UK, US, Canada, Germany and Ireland.* San Antonio, TX: Psychological Corporation.

5 Self meets the environment

In this chapter, two articles are presented that consider the way interactions between some mental and neurophysiological attributes of ourselves, and certain characteristics of the environment, can affect aspects of our health and sense of well-being. You will probably have experienced that stress, anxiety, mood and depression can be triggered by external factors such as work, deadlines, turmoil with family or friends, finding a home or financial worries. They can also be triggered by internal factors such as what can be called outlook on life (are you a glass half-full or half-empty sort of person?), emotional state, neurotransmitter imbalances and, in the first article by Simor *et al.* (2011), sleep quality and the content of dreams. External factors from the environment can affect our internal well-being or state, and our internal well-being or state can affect our interactions with the environment. Most people, for example, have experienced disturbed sleep at some stage in their lives, and will know that it can provoke changes in mood, thought processes and your general appreciation of what is going on. Many reach for various solutions to minimise sleep's impact on their experiences and, consequentially, on their daily lives. Rather than resorting to medication, relaxation, meditation and mindfulness techniques have become popular alternatives.

The second article by Salvaia, Elias and Shepherd (2014) focuses on the effect of our visual environment on the experience of visual discomfort. Visual discomfort refers to the illusions, discomfort and pain that can be experienced when visual stimuli such as high-contrast stripes, glare and flicker are viewed. Their main focus was visual discomfort experienced by night-time taxi drivers from light emitting diodes (LEDs) that have been fitted to new cars recently. LEDs are bright, directional, point light sources, strung together on cars to make bright headlights (white), braking lights (red) and direction indicator lights (orange). A secondary question was whether the visual discomfort elicited by LEDs on cars was greater in drivers prone to headache and migraine. LEDs have been cropping up in many places on our roads and in our interiors; indeed, there are several cities that have introduced LEDs as the sole source of night-time lighting without due prior research, to the detriment of people and wildlife.

Simor, P., Köteles, F., Sándor, P., Petke, Z. & Bódizs, R. (2011) Mindfulness and dream quality: The inverse relationship between mindfulness and negative dream affect, *Scandinavian Journal of Psychology*, 52(4), pp. 369–375. doi: 10.1111/j.1467-9450.2011.00888.x.

Sleep disturbances are remarkably common: in the UK, the Sleep Council estimates 40% of people have sleep problems with consequences that range from contributing to road deaths to lack of productivity at work costing the economy billions.[1] Sleep disturbances involve the number of hours people spend asleep, whether sleep is unbroken or fitful, and whether sleep is refreshing. Dreams can affect the quality of sleep, particularly negative ones. Most people will have experienced anxiety dreams where their teeth fall out or where they are running to catch a train or bus, or running round in circles. These dreams are not particularly distressing, although you may wake feeling weary. Some dreams are benign but bizarre, such as dreaming that your cat is turning into a crocodile from the paws up. They can leave you bemused as to where the dreams came from, but they are not distressing. Most people will have also experienced nightmares, which can be sufficiently ghastly to awaken you. People typically do not wake from these dreams feeling refreshed. Mindfulness has become increasingly popular in recent years as a way to improve our outlook on ourselves and on the environment around us. Simor *et al.* examined whether mindfulness may have a positive effect on the content of dreams.

Synopsis

Introduction

Simor *et al.* (2011) begin with a summary of mindfulness whereby a person focuses their awareness on internal and external experiences in an open-minded, relaxed and non-judgemental way. It is a frame of mind a person can adopt, akin to a peaceful observer who deliberately contemplates what is going on around them and what they are experiencing in themselves, but without acting on those experiences at that moment in time. They continue with some examples showing mindfulness to be beneficial in a range of conditions, both clinical and non-clinical, such as stress reduction, improved mood and other 'psychopathological' conditions. For the latter they cite Roemer *et al.* (2009), who address the effects of mindfulness on generalised anxiety disorder and difficulties in regulating emotion. They mention positive effects of mindfulness training in non-clinical settings, including sleep *quality* and a sense of well-being. They cite several studies that have shown relationships between sleep quality, mindfulness, enhanced attentional processing, emotion regulation and cognitive flexibility. Here Simor *et al.* want to extend previous research by looking at the emotional *content* of dreams.

There then follows a section on REM sleep, consolidation of emotional memories and dreaming. They suggest the content of dreams is dictated by emotional issues and concerns that arise when awake. Specifically, they propose positive dream content has been associated with positive well-being, whereas nightmares are associated with psychopathological conditions such as depression, anxiety, schizophrenia, post-traumatic stress disorder and/or personality disorders. They summarise this section by characterising disturbed dreaming with two overarching components: negative dream quality itself (unpleasant dreams with or without awakenings) and dream anxiety (emotional and cognitive difficulties when awake following unpleasant dreams).

Simor *et al.* provide four hypotheses. The first three refer to disturbed dreaming. The aspects of disturbed dreaming they focus on are negative dream quality and anxiety, when awake, that stems from negative dreams (termed waking dream anxiety).

1 Disturbed dreaming will have a positive association, and mindfulness a negative association, with trait-like anxiety and state-like perceived stress.
2 Mindfulness will be associated with less severe dream disturbances.
3 Mindfulness will moderate the relationship between trait anxiety and disturbed dreaming. Consequently, the interaction between mindfulness and trait anxiety will be associated with the level of dream disturbances.
4 Mindfulness will moderate the relationship between negative dream quality and waking dream anxiety.

> *These are all directional hypotheses. Most are really a number of hypotheses (see GQ1).*
> *The issue of moderation will be addressed in GQ6.*

Methods

Simor *et al.* recruited 587 Psychology undergraduates (162 females, 425 males) with a mean age of 20.6 ± 2.2 years. The students were told the study was to investigate the relationship between sleep, dreaming and personality.

> *It is not ideal to tell participants the relationships between the variables that you are interested in (that knowledge may affect their responses or behaviour: demand characteristics, see Chapter 2). On the other hand, it would be fairly obvious to the students what the study was about from the content of the questionnaires. It is notable that they had so many males in their sample and that the age range is so restricted. Might this affect the data they have collected?*

The authors used the trait anxiety component of the State-Trait Anxiety Inventory (STAI-T; Spielberger, Corsuch & Lusgene, 1970); the Perceived Stress Scale (PSS; Cohen, Kamarck & Mermelstein, 1983); the Dream Quality Questionnaire (DQQ; Bódizs *et al.*, 2008); the Van Dream Anxiety Scale (VDAS) to assess anxiety, when awake, from negative or frightening dreams (Agargun, Kara & Bilici, 1999); and the Mindful Attention Awareness Scale (MAAS; Brown & Ryan, 2003). They cite internal consistency for each scale as moderate to high (the lowest Cronbach alpha was 0.55 for the DQQ, the highest 0.91 for the VDAS). The study was completed on-line using standard questionnaires, translated into Hungarian.

It is curious that the authors did not also assess sleep quality. There is a Sleep Quality Scale (Yi, Shin & Shin, 2006), referenced in one of their citations (Howell et al., 2008), which assesses several areas: 'daytime dysfunction, restoration after sleep, difficulty in falling asleep, difficulty in getting up, satisfaction with sleep, and awaking during sleep' (2008, p. 775). It is plausible that these factors would affect daytime anxiety, stress, dream quality, dream anxiety and success at being able to achieve a positive mindful state.

All except the DQQ are measured with rating scales. Total scores for each participant were calculated by summing the scale items for the PSS, STAI and VDAS. (There were two stages of summing for the VDAS. Question 5 of the VDAS has 12 sub-questions relating to the following symptoms when awake: dizziness, palpitations, sweating, shivering, shortness of breath, exhaustion, nausea, stomach aches, tightness in the chest, dry mouth, sore throat and fear of death. These are summed separately and re-coded into categories depending on how frequently the symptoms are reported using a 5-point scale ranging from 0 to 4. These new scores are then summed together with the responses to the other questionnaires.) The MAAS is usually scored by calculating the mean of its 15 questions; however, Simor et al. instead summed the responses for each participant. Summing or averaging is unlikely to make a great deal of difference. The DQQ is scored by summing component loadings following a principal components analysis (Bódizs et al., 2008).

Simor et al. used only those questions from the DQQ that related to negative emotional aspects of dreaming. The DQQ has rating scales with four categories: 'usually', 'frequently', 'rarely', 'never'. This part of the scale addresses things such as how frequently the emotional content of one's dreams is expressly oppressive and bad, or how frequently the emotional load of one's dreams is bad. Other parts of the DQQ have just 'yes/no' answers. For example, waking up startled out of sleep, sweating, fluttering and not knowing where you are.

The MAAS asks respondents to answer the questions using a 6-point scale with categories: 'almost always', 'very frequently', 'somewhat frequently', 'somewhat infrequently', 'very infrequently', 'almost never'. Questions address difficulty staying focused on what is happening in the present; doing jobs or tasks automatically, without being aware of what one is doing; being preoccupied with the present or the past; not noticing feelings of physical tension or discomfort until they really grab your attention.

The VDAS has a series of questions on sleep and dreams (e.g. 'During the last month, how often have you had a frightening dream and awaken completely from it?') and questions on general well-being related to frightening dreams (e.g. 'During the past month, how often have you had the following symptoms because of your frightening dreams?', e.g. dizziness, palpitations, sweating, tightness in chest, fear of death). All VDAS questions are rated on a 5-point scale: 'never', 'rarely', 'sometimes', 'usually', 'often'.

The STAI-T items include 'I am content' and 'I worry too much over something that doesn't matter', each rated on a 4-point scale with response possibilities 'almost always', 'often', 'sometimes', 'almost never'.

The PSS has items such as 'In the last month, how often have you felt that you were unable to control the important things in your life?', 'In the last month, how often have you felt nervous and "stressed"?', 'In the last month, how often have you felt that things were going your way?'. Each question is rated on a 5-point scale: 'never', 'almost never', 'sometimes', 'fairly often', 'very often'.

Recap: Level of measurement. When Likert-type rating scales are used, with scale endpoints 'agree' or 'disagree' and 5–7 gradations in-between, they are commonly accepted as interval (see Chapter 2). Most of the questionnaires used by Simor et al., however, comprise ordinal – not interval – scales, yet the instructions for scoring each questionnaire treat the data as interval. You could criticise anyone who creates a mean, or sums responses, from ordinal rating scales, as this is inappropriate; however, if the instructions for use of each scale stipulate that the ratings should be averaged or summed ... the criticism lies with the creators of the scales.

Simor *et al.* do not mention in what order the questionnaires were administered, or how long the session took, on average. The students had to complete over 70 questions. Time to complete, order of presentation, and missing data when questions are not answered are important considerations, particularly when the testing was done on-line so no-one could monitor diligence or attention over the duration of the session. Given the large number of questions to complete or rate, boredom or fatigue may have affected later answers. There inevitably is missing data with on-line studies, but the authors did not say what they did if students failed to answer particular questions. This is particularly important for those scales where the total score is calculated by summing the response to each scale item. Summation would be affected if it were based on, for example, 16 items rather than the full 20 for the STAI-T. The same comment applies for the PSS, VDAS and MAAS. If there are not too many missing answers, a common solution is to replace the missing question with an average (the mean, median or mode) from the rest of the responses to that question. If one person has failed to answer many of the questions, the best solution is to exclude their data completely.

It is perhaps an omission not to have asked the students if they had prior experience of mindfulness or meditation, since that could skew their responses compared with naive participants.

Results

Simor *et al.* first ran Kendall's tau correlation coefficients (τ) between all variables. All were statistically significant, although the correlations, on the whole, were quite modest, ranging from 0.17 (MAAS vs. DQQ, $\tau = -0.17$; PSS vs. VDAS, $\tau = 0.17$) to 0.51 (STAI-T vs. PSS). They ran Kendall's tau, a non-parametric test, as the data from two of the scales were not normally distributed, but Simor *et al.* do not say which two scales. Kendall's tau is calculated on ranked data, not the actual scores. They highlight the correlations of most interest. First, that trait anxiety and perceived stress were positively associated with dream disturbances: those with higher trait anxiety ratings also had higher perceived stress and higher negative dream experiences. Second, that mindfulness was negatively associated with trait anxiety, perceived stress, negative dream quality and waking dream anxiety: those with higher mindfulness ratings reported lower trait anxiety, stress, negative dream quality and waking dream anxiety.

Having declared that the data from two of the scales were not normally distributed, Simor *et al.* nevertheless proceed with three moderated hierarchical linear regression analyses. Some of the assumptions required for hierarchical linear regression are: the dependent variable should be measured at an interval or ratio level; there should be a linear relationship between the dependent and independent variable(s), which can be gauged with a scatterplot; there should be no significant outliers; the data should be homoscedastic for all independent and moderator variables (the variance around the regression line should be similar for each combination of the independent and moderator variables); there should not be multicollinearity within the independent variables (they should not be highly intercorrelated); and there should not be much missing data. It is impossible to judge these requirements from the information provided.

> Simor et al. do not provide scatterplots for any of their correlations, or mention whether there were any outliers. Although the correlations are reported to be significant for the ranked data, the actual scores would have been used in the regression analyses rather than the ranked scores.
>
> The range of mean scores for each scale is large, as are several standard deviations, which is some cause for concern (means $\pm$ 1 standard deviation): MAAS, 56.9 $\pm$ 9.2; VDAS, 6.1 $\pm$ 7.2; DQQ, 6.6 $\pm$ 1.3; STAI-T, 42.9 $\pm$ 9.2; PSS, 26.7 $\pm$ 7.3. From these, it is likely that the VDAS was one of the scales not normally distributed (look at the size of the standard deviation relative to the mean), yet it was used as a dependent variable in the second and third regression analyses.
>
> For the STAI-T, scores can range from 0 to 80. For the PSS, the range is 0 to 40. For the VDAS, the range is 0 to 42 (Agargun et al., 1999), although Simor et al. report the scale to range from 0 to 52. For the MAAS, the range is 1 to 90. It is impossible to tell the range of scores for the DQQ, as it is based on component weightings following a principal components analysis and will differ for different samples.

To resolve the issue that the scales had different ranges, Simor *et al.* centred the STAI-T and MAAS scores before proceeding with their first two analyses. Centring involves subtracting a value, usually the mean, from each score. If the mean is used, centring results in the new mean being zero for each scale but the distribution of scores around the mean is not affected. It is a way to standardise the scores when they have very different mean values. Centring allowed Simor *et al.* to create an interaction term (STAI-T scores multiplied by MAAS scores for each participant for their first two regression analyses) and, by including both the individual scores and their interaction term, they hoped to be able to tease apart the contribution of each in the analyses.

The first analysis used negative dream quality (DQQ) as the dependent variable, and the predictor variables were gender, perceived stress (PSS), trait anxiety (STAI-T), mindfulness (MAAS) and the interaction term, entered into the analysis in that order. All except PSS and the interaction term were significant predictors of the dream quality scores. They settled on a model that included gender, STAI-T and MAAS as predictors of poor sleep quality (model 4 of 5). The cumulative R^2 equalled 0.15, accounting for 15% of the variance in the dream quality data.

> There is no explanation why the predictor variables were entered in this order.

The second analysis used dream anxiety (VDAS) as the dependent variable and the same predictor variables. All except perceived stress were significant predictors of the dream anxiety scores. The cumulative R^2 for the final model again equalled 0.15, accounting for 15% of the variance in the dream anxiety data.

For the third analysis, the authors centred the data for poor dream quality (DQQ) and mindfulness (MAAS), and created a new interaction term, DQQ scores multiplied by MAAS scores for each participant. Dream anxiety (VDAS) was again the dependent variable. Gender, perceived stress and trait anxiety were now dropped from the analysis and only negative dream quality, mindfulness and the interaction term between them were used as predictors. Only negative dream quality and mindfulness were significant predictors of dream anxiety; the interaction term was not. Thus, model 2 (of 3) was selected and accounted for 32% of the variance in the dream anxiety data.

Conclusions

Simor *et al.* conclude that their results are consistent with earlier research showing a relationship between mindfulness, anxiety and sleep. They consider that they have extended previous research on sleep and mindfulness into the area of dream content.

They start their discussion by commenting on the significant correlations between all six of the questionnaire scales that were consistent with previous research. Mindfulness was negatively associated with dream quality, dream anxiety, perceived stress and trait anxiety: if you have low mindfulness scores, you are likely to score highly on the dream disturbance scales, stress and trait anxiety, and vice versa. Conversely, the other scales all correlated positively with each other: for example, if you score highly on trait anxiety, you are likely to score highly on the negative dream scales and on perceived stress. They then repeat the results of the regression analyses.

From the first regression analysis, the authors conclude that mindfulness and trait anxiety predicted negative dream *quality*, but their interaction did not, which they suggest indicates that the effects of mindfulness and trait anxiety act independently on dream quality.

From the second regression analysis (where dream *anxiety* was the dependent variable), as with negative dream *quality*, those with higher mindfulness scores experienced less dream anxiety, whereas those reporting high trait anxiety also had higher dream anxiety. Simor *et al.* suggest the significant interaction term (trait anxiety and mindfulness) may indicate that increased mindfulness moderates the negative influence of trait anxiety and results in reduced dream anxiety.

From the third regression analysis, the authors hoped to explore the interaction between dream quality, dream anxiety and mindfulness. The dependent variable was again dream anxiety. Dream quality was a significant predictor of dream anxiety, as was mindfulness but not the interaction between them.

Simor *et al.* end with a lengthy section on possible mechanisms and the possible relevance of REM sleep. They raise several avenues for future research including testing groups other than university students. They suggest testing individuals who train in meditation, individuals who are lucid dreamers and individuals with post-traumatic stress disorder, as mindfulness may be more effective with these groups. They refer to possible difficulties and limitations running on-line studies. They further comment on possible vagaries introduced using retrospective self-report and discuss, for future research, prospective longitudinal studies involving sleep logs and mindfulness training, which may give more reliable data. They also suggest the use of different methodologies (fMRI, EEG). It is only in the last paragraph of their Discussion that they reflect on how well the scales they used map onto what they wanted to study. That is, the concepts they wanted to study are clear, but did they operationalise them well with their choice of scales? (See Chapter 2 for a discussion of conceptional and operational definitions of variables.) Simor *et al.* specifically mention low internal validity for the dream quality scale, of which they only used the negative questions. The authors also mention an issue they had raised in the Introduction: that there are various ways to measure mindfulness, which consists of several components, yet they chose a scale that assesses just one dimension of mindfulness.

The ten general questions (10GQs)

This article has not yet been used in class, it was set in the 2021 exam. See Chapter 8 for example answers to the exercises and a standalone critique.

1(a). Does the report specify an hypothesis? If so, what is it? Is there more than one? As mentioned in the synopsis, the authors provide four directional hypotheses, but many are compound, making eleven explicit hypotheses:

1 Negative dream quality will be positively associated with trait anxiety.
2 Negative dream quality will be positively associated with perceived stress.
3 Dream anxiety will be positively associated with trait anxiety.
4 Dream anxiety will be positively associated with perceived stress.
5 Mindfulness will be negatively associated with trait anxiety.
6 Mindfulness will be negatively associated with perceived stress.
7 Mindfulness will be negatively associated with negative dream quality.
8 Mindfulness will be negatively associated with dream anxiety.
9 Mindfulness will moderate (ameliorate) the association between trait anxiety and dream quality.
10 Mindfulness will moderate (ameliorate) the association between trait anxiety and dream anxiety.

Hypotheses 7 and 8 use an interaction term derived from the measures of mindfulness and trait anxiety.

11 Mindfulness will moderate (ameliorate) the association between dream quality and dream anxiety.

Two of the regression analyses included gender, therefore Simor *et al.* must have considered there to be a gender difference, leading to two further implicit hypotheses:

12 Gender will predict dream quality.
13 Gender will predict dream anxiety.

1(b). What background or rationale is provided as justification for any hypothesis? Simor *et al.* cite relevant previous research on mindfulness and its relationship with emotional control, stress reduction, personality traits, anxiety, cognitive flexibility, attention, sleep quality and well-being. They also cite previous work that has examined the relationships several of these items have with clinical and psychopathological conditions. Dream content, particularly disturbing dreams and nightmares, has been examined before, but they consider that the effects of a positive mental attitude – such as having a mindful outlook – on dream content, dream quality, anxiety and stress have not been examined to date. The literature is mostly relevant, though the section is a little lengthy and at times repetitive.

2(a). Specify all the variables in the investigation and indicate what sort of variables they are (e.g. dependent vs. independent,

manipulated, controlled, nuisance, confounding). **Specify what level of measurement has been achieved for each dependent variable (nominal, ordinal, interval, ratio).** Simor *et al.* have five dependent variables:

1 Mindfulness, measured with the Mindfulness Attention Awareness Scale (MAAS; Brown & Ryan, 2003).
2 Trait anxiety, measured with the trait component of the State-Trait Anxiety Inventory (STAI-T; Spielberger *et al.*, 1970).
3 Negative dream quality, measured with the negative items from the Dream Quality Questionnaire (DQQ; Bódizs *et al.*, 2008).
4 Waking dream anxiety, measured by the Van Dream Anxiety Scale (VDAS; Agargun *et al.*, 1999).
5 Perceived Stress Scale (PSS; Cohen *et al.*, 1983).

All are measured using rating scales (see synopsis). The authors do not mention if all the questionnaires were completed in the same order or if the order differed for different students. If they all completed the questionnaires in the same order, tiredness or boredom may have affected their motivation or diligence when filling out the later questionnaires, constituting a nuisance variable.

They also included gender, a natural variable, coded into female and male categories. Age is a controlled variable, since all participants were recruited from an introductory psychology course, and there is a limited age range (20.59 ± 2.2 years). There are many more males (426) than females (162), making gender a nuisance variable. They also tested psychology students and some of them may have come across these questionnaires already in class (particularly the trait anxiety scale, STAI-T), making another nuisance variable.

2(b). Do the selected variables address the research hypothesis/ hypotheses? The content of the questionnaires does address most aspects of their hypotheses. They have chosen previously used scales, some more familiar than others, which address the different multiple components of dreams, anxiety, stress and mindfulness. While mindfulness may be multi-faceted, they justified the use of the MAAS because it addresses mindfulness, without including emotions or emotional regulation, it measures 'a receptive attentional stance toward inner and outer present moment experiences' (2011, p. 369). They mention most scales had acceptable internal consistency. In the Introduction, the authors make a reasonable case for the inclusion of each questionnaire, and at the end acknowledge some limitations: the DQQ has low internal reliability despite having reasonable internal consistency, and they recommend that future research should assess dream quality with other measures. They comment on the limited scope of MAAS to assess mindfulness, as it taps just one dimension, and recommend that future research should examine the effects of other components of mindfulness on dreaming.

3. What did the participants have to do? (briefly) Is the study easily replicable? This study was conducted on-line. Enough detail is provided on the questionnaires used to allow replication, except for not knowing which questions from the Dream Quality Questionnaire were used.

4(a). What experimental design was used? This study used a correlational design.

4(b). Do the method and design address the research hypothesis/ hypotheses? The method and design do address their research hypotheses, with the caveat that we do not know in what order the questionnaires were administered to each participant. As mentioned above, if they were presented all in the same order, then tiredness or boredom may have affected how diligently they responded to the later questionnaires. Consequently, the questionnaires would not accurately capture the dimension they were hoping to capture.

On-line studies notoriously result in data where the participants can rush through, skip questions and, in my experience, appear to press keys randomly. It is better to test people, even in groups, with someone in the room to be able identify those rushing through, getting bored, sighing, sleeping (!), taking breaks or being interrupted by family members, friends or pets. Otherwise, it is a waste of their time and yours (their reward was course credits, which they would have obtained regardless of how diligently they responded). As mentioned in earlier chapters, there are also people who like to give socially desirable answers, others who will try to scupper a study, and still others who may be embarrassed to answer some of the questions. Simor *et al.* do not mention any steps taken to discard outliers or nonsense. They also do not say what they did with missing data. One way to deal with missing data is to replace that entry with a group average (mean, median or mode), which is better than leaving one question blank and, if it is needed to be done only infrequently, will not have much of an impact on the data as a whole. If missing data are not replaced, the overall score for that scale, which is the sum of responses to each scale item, could be severely underestimated. As mentioned in the synopsis, anyone with very incomplete answers should be excluded.

5. What comparisons were chosen for statistical analysis? Simor *et al.* examined the correlations between all five scale responses, making 11 correlations. They also ran three hierarchical regressions to determine which variables predicted negative dream quality and dream anxiety.

6. What analysis was used? Was it appropriate? The authors used Kendall's tau correlation coefficient (τ) to assess the correlations between all pairs of variables, which is used on ranked data. This is appropriate, since they mention the results from two of the scales were not normally distributed. From the table of correlations presented, at least one of these scales would be the dream anxiety scale (VDAS), as the standard deviation (7.1) is larger than the mean (6.05, giving a coefficient of variation $(CV)^2$ of 116%); the second scale may be the perceived stress scale, as it has a relatively large standard deviation (7.16) compared to the mean (27.7, giving the next highest CV of 27%).

Simor *et al.* then conducted three stepwise hierarchical regressions. For the first, the dependent variable was negative dream quality. Gender was inserted in the first step, perceived stress in the second step, trait anxiety in the third, mindfulness in the fourth and an interaction term in the fifth: a combination of the data from the mindfulness and trait anxiety scales. They did not explain why they entered these variables in the order they did other than to say it would provide 'a conservative method calculating the independent power of mindfulness on negative dream quality, after controlling for the predictive power of gender, perceived stress, and trait anxiety' (2011, p. 372). To create the interaction term, the authors centred the mindfulness and trait anxiety scores by subtracting the mean from each score so that the new mean was zero for each scale, but the distribution of scores around zero was not affected. They then multiplied the centred scores together, for each participant, to create a new interaction variable, the product of STAI-T and mindfulness.

They repeated the same regression model in a second hierarchical regression analysis using dream anxiety as the dependent variable.

For the third regression analysis, dream anxiety was again the dependent variable, but gender, perceived stress and trait anxiety were not included. Dream quality was inserted in the first step, mindfulness in the second and a new interaction term in the third: a combination of the data from the mindfulness and dream quality scales. The data from both scales were centred, as before, to create a new interaction variable, the product of mindfulness and dream quality.

These analyses are appropriate for the research questions they wanted to ask, although some justification for the order of variables introduced at each step would have been useful. One might suppose they left the most interesting variables until last (trait anxiety, mindfulness and their interaction).

7. What was the main result? The correlations were as expected from previous research.

Mindfulness questionnaire data (MAAS) correlated negatively with the data from all of the other questionnaires: those with higher mindfulness scores had lower trait anxiety (STAI-T), dream anxiety (VDAS), perceived stress (PSS) and negative dream quality ratings (DQQ).

Conversely, dream anxiety correlated positively with negative dream quality, trait anxiety and perceived stress: those who scored highly on dream anxiety also scored highly on negative dream quality, trait anxiety and perceived stress.

Negative dream quality correlated positively with trait anxiety and perceived stress: those who scored highly on negative experiences of dream quality scored highly on trait anxiety and perceived stress.

Trait anxiety correlated positively with perceived stress: those who scored highly on trait anxiety also scored highly on perceived stress.

Simor *et al.* assessed negative dream quality as the dependent variable in the first hierarchical regression analysis; gender, perceived stress, trait anxiety, mindfulness and the interaction between trait anxiety and mindfulness were entered into the analysis in that order. As mentioned in the synopsis, they selected a model that included gender, trait anxiety and mindfulness as significant predictors of poor dream quality. The cumulative R^2 equalled 0.15, accounting for 15% of the variance in the dream quality data. Interestingly, the addition of mindfulness at step 4 affected the contribution of perceived stress: it had been a significant predictor of poor dream quality in the earlier models (steps 2 and 3) but was no longer so when mindfulness was added. This point is not commented upon, yet it could be interpreted as the effect of stress being moderated by the stronger effect of mindfulness. This may indicate multicollinearity, since mindfulness and stress were significantly intercorrelated ($\tau = -0.29$), which is not ideal for multiple regression, but it is nevertheless interesting, since it shows the relative importance of mindfulness over stress. Mindfulness eclipses stress.

In the second regression analysis, the dependent variable was dream anxiety; gender, perceived stress, trait anxiety, mindfulness and the interaction between trait anxiety and mindfulness were again entered into the analysis in that order. Four predictor variables were retained in the final model: gender, trait anxiety, mindfulness and the interaction between trait anxiety and mindfulness. This model also accounted for 15% of the variance in the dream anxiety data. Perceived stress had been a significant predictor when added at step 2, but it was no longer so once trait anxiety had been added to the model at step 3. This again could be evidence of multicollinearity, as the correlation between trait anxiety and stress was relatively large ($\tau = 0.51$). Yet again this is interesting, since it could indicate stress – as measured by the perceived stress scale – is subsumed by trait anxiety.

The third regression had a simper structure: dream anxiety was the dependent variable and only poor dream quality, mindfulness and their interaction were entered into the analysis, in that order. Only poor dream quality and mindfulness predicted dream anxiety, and the model accounted for 32% of the variance in the dream anxiety data.

8. What conclusions were drawn? Were they valid? Simor *et al.* state that the significant intercorrelations between all of the variables are in line with previous research. The most relevant results were: (1) the significant negative correlations between mindfulness and the other variables – those with high mindfulness scores tended to have lower trait anxiety, perceived stress, less poor quality dreams and less dream anxiety; (2) the

significant positive correlations between all variables except mindfulness – those high in trait anxiety tended to have higher perceived stress,
greater negative dream quality and higher dream anxiety.

Following the first regression analysis (where negative dream *quality*
was the dependent variable), they conclude that females and more anxious people experience poorer dream quality. Mindfulness and trait
anxiety scores also predicted poor dream quality when entered independently (negative and positive significant *b* coefficients, respectively):
those with higher mindfulness scores endorsed fewer items on a questionnaire that describes unpleasant dreams, whereas those who reported
higher trait anxiety also gave higher ratings of negative dream quality.
Since the interaction term (trait anxiety and mindfulness) was not a significant predictor of dream quality – whereas when entered in separate
steps, trait anxiety and mindfulness were – they conclude the effects of
mindfulness and trait anxiety on dream *quality* are independent.

From the second regression analysis (where dream *anxiety* was the
dependent variable), their model again indicates that females and more
anxious people reported greater dream anxiety. As with negative dream
quality, when mindfulness and trait anxiety were entered separately
into the analysis, both significantly predicted dream anxiety (significant
negative and positive *b* coefficients, respectively): those with higher
mindfulness scores experienced less dream anxiety, whereas those
reporting high trait anxiety also had higher dream anxiety on a scale
where higher scores mean more anxiety.

Moreover, that the interaction term (trait anxiety and mindfulness) significantly predicted dream anxiety was interpreted as showing that higher
levels of mindfulness were associated with dream anxiety when all the
other variables are equal (the *b* coefficient was small, but statistically significant). The authors suggest that increased mindfulness may moderate
the effects of trait anxiety and so reduce dream anxiety. This interpretation
of the interaction term is not explained clearly. Perhaps they reached this
conclusion because the association between dream anxiety and mindfulness was negative ($b = -0.210$), the association between dream anxiety
and trait anxiety was positive ($b = 0.217$), while the association between
dream anxiety and the interaction term was much smaller and negative ($b
= -0.084$), thus the interaction term was dominated by the mindfulness
scores rather than the trait anxiety scores. Simor *et al.* comment that
because the interaction term only significantly predicted dream *anxiety*,
not dream *quality*, dream anxiety and dream quality are related but not
equivalent constructs. They suggest this conclusion is bolstered by the
results of the third regression. They also conclude that mindfulness does
not moderate waking anxiety about dreaming.

9. What are your main criticisms of the report? The authors have
tried to weave together a fairly complicated set of analyses and the
overall conclusions, if convoluted, do follow from the analyses performed. Main issues include:

1 It would have been useful to have had more discussion on multicollinearity and more explanation of the moderation revealed by the interaction term in the second regression analysis.

2 Scatterplots, effect sizes and confidence intervals would have helped the reader grasp for themselves the nature of the results and the meaning of the one significant interaction term.

3 There are no comments about the distribution of the residuals: these should be normally distributed.

4 The report is very dense and difficult to follow in places. There is also a great deal of repetition throughout the manuscript. The Introduction and Discussion are lengthy and they bring in many tangential issues that at times muddy their arguments rather than extend them. There is unnecessary speculation, such as extending the work to lucid dreaming, and the discussion on fMRI, EEG and REM sleep is also tangential.

5 They end their discussion with speculation on possible mechanisms underlying the inverse associations between mindfulness and disturbed dreaming. The discussion overgeneralises mindfulness at the expense of trait anxiety: they place a great deal of emphasis on the second regression where the interaction between mindfulness and trait anxiety did significantly add to the model predicting dream anxiety. An example of this overgeneralisation is that, when discussing possible clinical applications of these results, they claim that mindfulness predicted both dream anxiety and dream quality above and beyond trait anxiety, whereas it did not.

6 The description of the questionnaires was a little brief, unless the reader knows them, which makes it difficult for the reader to evaluate their appropriateness for themselves.

7 It would have been useful also to have a measure of sleep quality and quantity, as this intuitively seems likely to affect dream quality and quantity (see synopsis for suggested parameters that could have been included).

8 There are several personal details about their students that they could have added, which might have affected their results: the students' lifestyle, their typical sleeping habits, use of alcohol or drugs, and whether they had prior experience with mindfulness or meditation.

10. What are the main strengths of the report? The study set up by Simor *et al.* is interesting and remains apposite in today's pandemic climate. The sample size is impressive, so there are no issues regarding power. The study was well thought out, its limitations noted, and sensible suggestions were made for future research (see synopsis for examples). Although the Introduction was lengthy with some tangential issues, they succinctly summarise most of their hypotheses at the end. The literature review is comprehensive, and the results obtained are tied back to existing literature in the Discussion.

Exercises

1   In the justification for their study, do the authors successfully weave together their discussion of mindfulness, sleep quality, cognitive behaviour therapy for insomnia, nightmares, waking well-being and psychopathological conditions? Is their suggestion of protective factors overcoming dream disturbances thereby plausible? How many hypotheses were presented? Evaluate the measures used and their appropriateness to address their research hypotheses.

2   Are the data presented clearly? Which analyses were used and were all of them necessary? Is the introduction of gender into the analyses justified, or the interaction term between STAIT and MAAS when each was also entered separately into the analyses? Comment on the conclusions that were drawn. In research like this, would it be useful to control for previous experience in meditation, mindfulness or yoga training?

Salvaia, J., Elias, S. & Shepherd, A. J. (2014) Symptoms of visual discomfort from automobile lights and their correlation with headache in night-time taxi drivers, *Lighting Research and Technology*, 46(3), pp. 354–363. doi: 10.1177/1477153513496782.

Many aspects of the environment can affect a person's comfort and health, yet they are not always adequately recognised by those who create the spaces in which we live and work. The environment can affect a person's comfort and sense of well-being by, for example, having a negative impact on mood, arousal, stress or the ability to concentrate. It can have more serious effects if it elicits discomfort or affects a person's health by aggravating existing conditions such as migraine, epilepsy, lupus, chronic fatigue or autism/Asperger's syndrome. Given the push for energy efficiency, LEDs (light emitting diodes) have become the preferred choice for lighting. They may be efficient, but they have downsides as well. They are bright, directional point sources, often strung together to create lighting strips, surfaces or more complicated arrays. Salvaia *et al.* (2014) highlight an evolving issue since the roll-out of LED lighting in our indoor and outdoor environments. They assess LEDs used on vehicles as rear, front and direction indicator lights. They focus specifically on visual discomfort, headache and night-time driving, and ask whether there is an increased risk of headache with the use of LEDs on cars.

Synopsis

Introduction

Salvaia *et al.* (2014) begin with a review of the complex demands involved in driving, particularly night-time driving, and the competing requirements for comfort, minimising discomfort, yet maintaining visibility for all road users. Driving is a highly complex skill requiring the sustained monitoring and integration of multiple visual, perceptual and cognitive processes and, when it goes wrong, the consequences include fatalities. Driving performance has elicited a great deal of research interest over the years, although research on the road, rather than in laboratories, often follows the introduction of new technologies rather than precedes them. Salvaia *et al.* point out the importance of understanding the consequences of the changing driving environments that follow new technological advances, particularly how they affect the health of drivers. They focus on whether night-time drivers experience headache elicited by LEDs. Earlier research had concentrated on disability and discomfort glare when driving at night and the need to minimise both while maintaining road visibility. As LEDs are very bright, directional light sources, they can elicit both disability and discomfort glare. Salvaia *et al.* note that while there are regulations that dictate the positioning of LEDs on car exteriors, and these are tested in the factory, all it takes is for a car to be driving on a sloping surface and the light direction can then fail the agreed standards. Similarly, dirt on the casing or movement of the LEDs within the casing can scatter the light in unwanted directions.

> *Most people will have experienced disability glare at night, where bright lights dazzle and impair the visibility of objects. Discomfort glare, as the name implies, is less intense, but is unpleasant and the tendency is to wince and turn away.*

On cars, LEDs are usually configured as a strip: the rear braking lights can appear as a horizontal line at the top or bottom of the vehicle, or vertically along both sides. In other words, they can appear anywhere in the visual field, for variable periods of time, and can flash on and off depending on the braking manoeuvres of the car ahead. They are also used as lettering on road signs, traffic signals, road lighting and decoration on buildings. Having LEDs both on the side of the road and on vehicles can result in them appearing suddenly anywhere, for various lengths of time, and they commonly flash on and off. Attention can be caught by bright lights appearing in the periphery, which can cause distraction while driving and impair performance.

When this study was conducted, LEDs had just recently been introduced. They replaced the older brake lights, but the headlights were predominantly still halogen or xenon lamps with a strip of LEDs added as daytime (and night-time) running lights beneath them, giving the appearance of an upside-down, bright, eyebrow. Now, LEDs are used as the principal headlight as well, at least on high-end models.

Salvaia *et al.* ask how modern vehicle lights affect night-time drivers. They focus on headache and visual discomfort, as there are multiple studies showing they can be triggered by glare and flashing lights (reviewed in Harle, Shepherd

& Evans, 2006; Shepherd, 2010). They note prevalence rates for migraine in the general population (one in nine) and that it can be triggered by visual stimuli in up to 60% of those affected.

Methods

Sylvaia *et al.* recruited 68 night-time taxi drivers in central London during the winter of 2011–12. Their mean age was 50.7 ± 11.4 years, their ages ranged from 23 to 78 years, and there were 67 males and one female. They were approached at taxi stands outside mainline railway stations and at cab shelters by two of the authors. They were handed a short questionnaire and a freepost envelope to return when completed, or they completed the questionnaire while waiting on the taxi rank.

> *When people think of ethical issues, they often just consider how participants in the research are treated. Ethics also apply to those conducting the research: the two researchers always worked together for their own safety, as they were standing around at railway stations in the evening.*

The questionnaire asked about the driver's assessment of problematic symptoms associated with LED lights while driving at night. They specifically asked about LEDs on cars around the headlights and as tail and indicator lights, although the authors acknowledge the participants may have provided responses to other types of vehicle lights as well. They assessed the perception of flicker, blurring, seeing double images of the LEDs, smearing of the LEDs into each other, glare, blinding or visual impairment, unease, discomfort and pain. Each was rated on a 5-point scale where 1 denoted 'no problem', 3 denoted a 'moderate problem' and 5 denoted a 'debilitating problem'. The participants then identified the colour and location of the LEDs that they found the most problematic. Lastly, they were asked whether they experienced intermittent, strong headaches or migraines.

Night-time taxi drivers were chosen on the assumption that they undertake above-average hours of night-time driving and may be more aware of the impact of the introduction of LED lights than intermittent night-time drivers. On average, they drove at night 27.7 hours per week.

Results

Salvaia *et al.* report glare to be the most commonly reported problem, followed by blinding or visual impairment, then blurring or seeing double images of the LEDs. Thirty-two drivers cited white LEDs around headlights as the most problematic, 29 cited the red LED braking lights. No-one found orange direction indicator lights to be problematic. Seven did not answer the question. The authors divided the participants into two: those reporting white or those reporting red LEDs as the most problematic. The red brake lights were judged to be significantly more glaring than white lights around the headlights (independent-samples t-tests). None of the other possible symptoms differed between the groups.

> Does 'no problem' (one end of the rating scale) indicate the absence of the symptom being measured, in the same way that zero seconds means the absence of time? Salvaia et al. clearly thought so. If you disagree, then the data are ordinal. The authors do not comment on whether their ratings were normally distributed or whether there was homogeneity of variance between the groups. They could have used non-parametric tests for this comparison, such as the Mann-Whitney U-test. Whichever test is used, the outcome is the same.

Salvaia *et al.* then divided the participants into two different groups: those who reported experiencing intermittent, strong headaches and/or migraines ($N = 20$) and those who did not ($N = 48$). Glare was the most problematic symptom for both groups.[3] 'A rating of 5 on the scale indicated a debilitating problem. In the headache group, 5 was the most frequent rating given for glare, blinding or visual impairment and discomfort, whereas it was the most frequent rating only for glare in the no-headache group. Modal ratings were calculated for each of the other possible symptoms (Table 5.1). The headache group gave higher ratings more frequently than the no-headache group for blinding or visual impairment, seeing double images of the LEDs, discomfort, experiencing flicker, and smearing of the LEDs into each other. A series of independent samples t-tests were performed: the headache group experienced significantly greater problems with discomfort, pain, unease, flickering and seeing double images, compared with the no-headache group. There were no differences in age or in the average number of hours driving at night per week between the groups.

> The visual aura is a set of transient visual symptoms that precede the headache and typically last for about half an hour. The classic aura is a series of zig-zag lines that start centrally and slowly move off to one side, leaving a scotoma (blindness) in its wake. Other visual symptoms can be experienced, such as seeing stars or phosphenes, or looking at the world as if through running water. Most involve visual impairment or transient blindness in one half of the visual field, and sometimes throughout the visual field. This is a troublesome report as there are clear safety issues involved: what did the drivers do while having an aura? Pull over?

Table 5.1 Medians and modes for each item rated on a 5-point scale, where 1 = 'no problem', 3 = 'moderate problem' and 5 = 'debilitating problem'

	Headache		No headache	
	Median	**Mode**	**Median**	**Mode**
Glare	4	5	4	5
Blinding or visual impairment	3.5	5	3	3
Blurring	3.5	4	3	4
Seeing double images of the LEDs	4	4	3	3
Unease	3	3	3	3
Discomfort	4	5	2	1
Flicker	3	4	3	1
Smearing of the LEDs into each other	3.5	4	2.5	1
Pain	2.5	1	1	1

The participants were asked to comment on the nature of the headaches they had while driving. Of the 20 who experienced severe headaches, six reported migraine (three with visual aura) and five reported experiencing headache commonly while driving at night and more commonly than during the day.

Salvaia *et al.* conducted a principal components analysis, with varimax rotation, to investigate associations between age, average hours a week of night-time driving, problematic symptoms and experiencing strong, intermittent headaches. The Kaiser-Meyer-Olkin measure (a measure of sampling adequacy) and Bartlett's test (of the strength of relationship between the variables) and the determinant score (a test of multicollinearity) indicated the data were suitable for this analysis. Three components were extracted, accounting for 68% of the variance in the original variables. Only those variables that had component loadings greater than 0.5 were retained. The three components were interpreted as:

1 A visual impairment component (comprising problematic symptoms of flickering, blurring, seeing double images of the LEDs, smearing of the LEDs into each other, blinding or visual impairment, unease, glare). All variables loaded positively onto this component and it accounted for 33% of the variance in the original variables.

2 A visual discomfort component (comprising unease, glare, discomfort, pain). Again, all variables loaded positively onto this component and it accounted for 22% of the variance in the original variables.

3 A personal component (comprising age, average hours driving at night, intermittent strong headaches while driving). Age had a negative loading on

the factor, hours driving at night and the experience of headache had positive loadings. This component accounted for 13% of the variance in the original variables. The change in sign of the loadings indicates younger drivers drove longer hours and were more likely to experience headaches at night while driving than older drivers.

Conclusions

Salvaia *et al.* conclude that a wide range of problematic effects are associated with LEDs when driving at night. Reports of glare were the most frequent of these effects and both red and white brake lights were equally frequently reported. Red braking lights were, however, rated as worse than the white LEDs around the headlights. Blurring, blinding or visual impairment, seeing double images of the LEDs and unease were the next most problematic symptoms. The headache group experienced greater problems, particularly for discomfort, blinding and visual impairment. These results are consistent with previous research on visually triggered headache and visual discomfort (Harle *et al.*, 2006; Shepherd, 2010).

The results supported the authors' expectation that vehicle lighting can lead to visual impairment when driving at night and that it can provoke unpleasant experiences of glare, unease and pain, which could affect driver performance. They also report that younger drivers drove longer hours at night and were more prone to night-time headaches, which was unexpected, as experiences of glare typically increase with age. The authors suggest that the older drivers had deliberately reduced the number of hours driving at night, perhaps because of glare and headache. They also point out that the younger drivers were not that young: the modal age was 45 years and the median was 50 years. They suggest that this may reflect the time it takes to learn 'the knowledge' to be a London taxi driver (on average, five years, but it can take longer).

Salvaia *et al.* end with a call for further research, as these effects have potentially dangerous ramifications for all night-time road users, especially given the increasing use of bright, directional LEDs on vehicles and on roadsides. As their research assessed city drivers, they suggest future research should assess motorway driving and other driving environments, such as country roads where there is less intrusion from other traffic, and roadside clutter, such as LED signs or decorations on buildings.

The authors suggest that one reason why the red braking lights were judged to be more glaring than the white lights may be due to city traffic: in London, the braking lights turn on and off repeatedly as the driver ahead crawls their way through the congested streets, whereas headlights are on continuously. The intermittent but repetitive braking is likely to be more intrusive than steady light from the headlights. They comment that the brake lights can be all over the rear of the car, and positioned higher up in the driver's line of sight, compared with headlights, which tend to be lower down in the visual field and in similar positions across different makes of cars. They suggest further extensions to the research, such as assessing the effects of LED usage on road signs, as road lighting, or as decoration on buildings and consequential experiences of glare, distraction and headache. Major roads are increasingly being cluttered with signs and the information they display often flashes. Salvaia *et al.* acknowledge the limitations of a brief questionnaire that was not completed face-to-face and recommend the design of a more detailed survey completed in person.

The ten general questions (10GQs)

This article has not been discussed in class.

1(a). Does the report specify an hypothesis? If so, what is it? Is there more than one? Salvaia *et al.* do not explicitly state an hypothesis because this was an exploratory study, but it can be inferred that they expected there would be an association between experiencing visual discomfort and LED vehicle lighting when driving at night and that discomfort would be greater in those prone to headache. It can also be inferred that the authors expected a difference in the experience of discomfort based on the colour and positioning of the LED lights on vehicles.

1(b). What background or rationale is provided as justification for any hypothesis? Based on prior research, Salvaia *et al.* compiled a list of likely problematic symptoms that drivers may experience at night: flicker, blurring, seeing double images of the LED lights, smearing of the LED lights into one another, glare, blinding or visual impairment, unease, discomfort, pain and headache. They also provided a background on prevalence rates of headache and migraine (one in nine people) and its disabling consequences. They cite the World Health Organisation that has ranked migraine 19th on their list of disability causes that impair a person's quality of life. The authors note that there are various headache and migraine triggers (stress, lack of sleep, tiredness, dehydration) but that visual stimuli such as glare and flicker have also been reported to be reliable migraine triggers in up to 60% of people with the condition (Shepherd, 2010). Finally, the selection of night-time taxi drivers was justified, as they spend more hours driving at night than others who tend to drive at night intermittently or for shorter periods of time.

2(a). Specify all the variables in the investigation and indicate what sort of variables they are (e.g. dependent vs. independent, manipulated, controlled, nuisance, confounding). Specify what level of measurement has been achieved for each dependent variable (nominal, ordinal, interval, ratio). There is no independent variable because this is an observational study. The dependent variables are the problematic symptoms. These were assessed using 5-point rating scales with endpoints 'no problem' and 'debilitating problem'. Salvaia *et al.* have taken these scales to yield interval or ratio data, on the assumption that if a person indicates they do not have a problem with, for example, glare, then that problem does not exist – that is, there is a true zero.

Headache was also assessed, and for the analyses, was used to allocate the participants into two groups. This is a natural, nominal/categorical variable. They were also allocated into groups according to whether they found the white headlights or the red brake lights the most problematic. This is a nominal/categorical variable.

Gender is a controlled variable, as all but one participant were male.

2(b). Do the selected variables address the research hypothesis/ hypotheses? The variables selected do cover the areas that the researchers wanted to explore. Salvaia *et al.* tested night-time taxi drivers, since they are a group likely to have experienced an impact of the introduction of LEDs on cars. The questionnaire asked about the taxi-drivers' experiences when exposed to LEDs on other cars and their experiences of headache and migraine (see the synopsis). The questionnaire specifically asked whether or not the driver found each symptom problematic, which may be considered leading, but this was considered to be circumnavigated by having one of the endpoints of each scale as 'not at all'.

3. What did the participants have to do? (briefly) Is the study easily replicable? Participants had to fill in a brief questionnaire and hand it back to the researchers, if there was time while they waited at a taxi rank, or post their questionnaires back in a freepost envelope. The study is replicable, since the questionnaire items are presented in enough detail that a comparable questionnaire could be constructed in future research.

4(a). What experimental design was used? This is an observational, correlational study.

4(b). Do the method and design address the research hypothesis/ hypotheses? Yes, the researchers wanted to explore the occurrence of problematic experiences and symptoms elicited by LED lighting on vehicles and designed a questionnaire to do so.

5. What comparisons were chosen for statistical analysis? The participants were first divided into two groups: those who found the white LEDs around headlights most problematic and those who found the red LED braking lights the most problematic. Differences in the ratings for each problematic symptom were then compared between these two groups.

The participants were then divided into two groups based on whether they reported experiencing intermittent, severe headaches. Differences in the ratings for each problematic symptom were then compared between these two groups.

Age and the average number of hours spent driving at night were compared for the two headache groups. Finally, the authors looked for associations between the variables age, average hours a week of night-time driving, headache, and the list of problematic symptoms.

6. What analysis was used? Was it appropriate? Salvaia *et al.* used independent-samples *t*-tests to compare the groups who found either the red or the white LED lights most intrusive, for each problematic symptom. Similarly, they used independent-samples *t*-tests to compare the headache and no-headache groups for each problematic symptom. The authors considered their data to be interval or ratio, but did not comment on whether the variance of ratings from each group was equivalent, or if the data were normally distributed, but note that the outcome is the same whether parametric or non-parametric tests were used for the group comparisons.

The authors used a principal components analysis to explore associations between the variables: age, average hours a week of night-time driving, headache, and the list of problematic symptoms. The data were suitable for this analysis if the data are considered interval or ratio. The data passed tests of multicollinearity (the determinant was greater than 0.00001), sampling adequacy (Kaiser-Meyer-Olkin measure greater than 0.5), and Bartlett's test for sphericity (for the strength of relationships between the variables, Bartlett's test <0.05), indicating that they were suitable for the analyses (Field, 2005).

7. What was the main result? Salvaia *et al.* found that red braking LED lights were more glaring than white LEDs around the headlights. They also found that people prone to severe headaches experienced significantly greater problems with discomfort, pain, unease, flickering and seeing double images, compared to those who were not prone to such headaches. The principal components analysis produced three components, interpreted as:

1 Visual impairment (comprising problematic symptoms of flickering, blurring, seeing double images of the LEDs, smearing of the LEDs into each other, blinding or visual impairment, unease, glare). All variables loaded positively onto this component. Positive loadings indicate that if you experience one of these symptoms, it is likely you experience the others.

2 Visual discomfort (comprising unease, glare, discomfort, pain). Again, all variables loaded positively onto this component, indicating that if you experience unease, you are likely to also experience glare, discomfort and pain.

3 Personal factors (comprising age, average hours driving at night, intermittent strong headaches while driving). Age had a negative loading on the factor, hours driving at night and the experience of headache had positive loadings, which they took to indicate that younger drivers drove longer hours at night and were more prone to night-time headaches.

8. What conclusions were drawn? Were they valid? Salvaia *et al.* concluded that night-time taxi drivers do indeed have negative experiences of LED lighting on vehicles, whether or not they experience intermittent, severe headaches, although the negative experiences were greater in the headache group. Glare was the greatest problem, and red braking LEDs were worse than white LEDs around the headlights. These conclusions follow from the data collected and from the analyses performed.

9. What are your main criticisms of the report?

1 The participants in this study came from an opportunity sample and the questionnaires were not administered face-to-face.

2 The study was restricted to night-time taxi drivers in central London, and all but one were male, so the generalisability of the work is limited to male taxi drivers driving in central London.

3 The participants were not particularly young, so further research is needed to include a wider age range and an even gender divide.

4 The questionnaire was necessarily short so that it could be completed at the kerbside, inside the black cab, and to maximise the likelihood that it would be completed and returned if filled in elsewhere. There is no control over where the questionnaire was completed if not at the kerbside.

5 The questionnaire could be considered to include leading questions: a longer version could be developed for the future that does not explicitly ask about problematic experiences when viewing LEDs (although the participants were able to select 'not at all').

10. What are the main strengths of the report? This was an innovative study motivated to understand hazards for night-time drivers from the introduction of LED lighting on vehicles. The results are consistent with previous studies of visual triggers of headache that have been conducted in the laboratory. The practical applications are clear and there are a number of extensions suggested for further research to widen the scope of research in this area.

Exercises

1 Have the authors made a compelling case to conduct their study? What did they study? Comment on the methods adopted and how suitable they are to address the issues of interest.

2 Are the data analysed satisfactorily? Comment on the statistics employed and the validity of the conclusions drawn. What further research do you see as being an important extension of this work?

Notes

1 https://sleepcouncil.org.uk/
2 The coefficient of variation (CV) is the standard deviation divided by the mean. It should really be used on ratio data, which has a meaningful zero (see Chapter 2 for further discussion on levels of measurement). Since Simor *et al.* are treating their data as interval by calculating means and standard deviations, I calculated CVs for illustration: sometimes you get an idea of information that is 'missing' in the printed article by extracting and further analysing what has been presented in the text, tables and graphs. The smaller the CV, the better the data, since it indicates little variation of scores around the mean, i.e. the mean is a good summary of the data on which it is based. Conversely, large CVs (and certainly those > 100%) indicate a great deal of variability around the mean and, therefore, the mean is not a good summary of the data it is supposed to summarise.
3 As only six drivers reported migraine out of the 20 who reported experiencing intermittent, strong headaches, Salvaia *et al.* combined the migraine and headache groups.

References

Agargun, M., Kara, H., Bilici, M. *et al.* (1999). The Van Dream Anxiety Scale: A subjective measure of dream anxiety in nightmare sufferers. *Sleep and Hypnosis, 1*(4), 204–211.

Bódizs, R., Simor, P., Csóka, S. *et al.* (2008). Dreaming and health promotion: A theoretical proposal and some epidemiological establishments. *European Journal of Mental Health, 3*(1), 36–62. https://doi.org/10.1556/EJMH.3.2008.1.3.

Brown, K. W., & Ryan, R. M. (2003). The benefits of being present: Mindfulness and its role in psychological well-being. *Journal of Personality and Social Psychology, 84*(4), 822–848. https://doi.org/10.1037/0022-3514.84.4.822.

Cohen, S., Kamarck, T., & Mermelstein, R. (1983). A global measure of perceived stress. *Journal of Health and Social Behavior, 24*(4), 385–396. https://doi.org/10.2307/2136404.

Field, A. P. (2005). *Discovering Statistics Using SPSS*, 2nd edn. London: Sage.

Harle, D. E., Shepherd, A. J., & Evans, B. J. W. (2006). Visual stimuli are common triggers of migraine and are associated with pattern glare. *Headache, 46*(9), 1431–1440. https://doi.org/10.1111/j.1526-4610.2006.00585.x.

Howell, A. J., Digdon, N. L., Buro, K. *et al.* (2008). Relations among mindfulness, well-being, and sleep. *Personality and Individual Differences, 45*(8), 773–777. https://doi.org/10.1016/j.paid.2008.08.005.

Roemer, L., Lee, J. K., Salters-Pedneault, K. *et al.* (2009). Mindfulness and emotion regulation difficulties in generalized anxiety disorder: Preliminary evidence for independent and overlapping contributions. *Behavior Therapy, 40*(2), pp. 142–154. https://doi.org/10.1016/j.beth.2008.04.001.

Salvaia, J., Elias, S., & Shepherd, A. J. (2014). Symptoms of visual discomfort from automobile lights and their correlation with headache in night-time taxi drivers. *Lighting Research and Technology, 46*(3), 354–363. https://doi.org/10.1177/1477153513496782.

Shepherd, A. J. (2010). Visual stimuli, light and lighting are common triggers of migraine and headache. *Journal of Light and Visual Environment, 34*(2), pp. 94–100. https://doi.org/10.2150/jlve.34.94.

Simor, P., Köteles, F., Sándor, P. *et al.* (2011). Mindfulness and dream quality: The inverse relationship between mindfulness and negative dream affect. *Scandinavian Journal of Psychology, 52*(4), 369–375. https://doi.org/10.1111/j.1467-9450.2011.00888.x.

Spielberger, C., Corsuch, R., & Lusgene, R. (1970) *Manual for the State-Trait Anxiety Inventory.* Palo Alto, CA: Consulting Psychologists Press.

Yi, H., Shin, K., & Shin, C. (2006) Development of the Sleep Quality Scale, *Journal of Sleep Research, 15*(3), 309–316. https://doi.org/10.1111/j.1365-2869.2006.00544.x.

6 The brief general critique

Most people would die sooner than think—in fact, they do so.

– Bertrand Russell

Sometimes I am asked, having completed the ten general questions (10GQs), and dug out the nuts and bolts or strengths and weaknesses of an article, what is the need for a separate critique? The answer is that it is good to fully understand an article, which you achieve having answered the 10GQs, but they are just the factual foundations of a piece of work. It is an invaluable skill to bring together the most salient points about an article and present them in a standalone critique. The 10GQs ensure you cover every aspect of an article and do not leave any issue out. You should look over your answers and decide which are the substantive points you have to make about an article and which are more trivial. The 10GQs give you the facts; the exercises you have been given after each article in Chapters 3–5 ask you to think about how to weave those facts together to form an argument, but still focusing on themes specific to the paper at hand. The critique is the essence of critical analysis. You should be able to create a balanced, standalone critique by the end of a degree.

There is no fixed agenda for a critique, as it depends on the strengths and weaknesses of the article you are assessing. A critique requires you to read an article and evaluate it: *every section*. You have to look at the details you have unearthed using the 10GQs, then analyse, reflect and come to your own conclusions about the article's strengths and weaknesses. Do not accept things the authors may say just because they have been printed – you need to judge if what has been said follows from the method and the data that have been presented.

Before you start a critique, you should sketch answers to the 10GQs: your answers to these questions give you the basics for a critique. Then you can consider the critique and use the mnemonic and acronym JARGON? to select several key issues or areas that are worth discussing. You need to decide whether the author's treatment of each issue or area is worth commenting on *either positively or negatively*. A critique does not mean negative criticism, you should try to find positive issues to discuss as well.

JARGON?

Justification: has a case been made for conducting the research?

Appropriate or ambitious? Can the research question be addressed with the particular method and design adopted? (i.e. no particulars on how the design is implemented yet, just consider whether the hypotheses could be answered with a design of the sort proposed).

Replicability: has sufficient detail been provided for someone else to repeat the study?

Generalisability:

- Adequate measures (conceptual vs. operational): do the measures chosen adequately measure what they are supposed to?
- Internal validity: is the internal logic of the research (design) satisfactory? Have the results been analysed correctly/thoroughly?
- External validity: how far can the results be generalised?

Organisation: this is of the written work, not the study.

- Have the authors presented their study in a well-organised, clear way and in sufficient detail?
- Are there serious flaws in the organisation or presentation of the paper (e.g. in language, format, tables or graphs)?
- Is the article complete? Are all relevant sections provided?

i**N**terpretation:

- Have the data and analyses been interpreted satisfactorily/correctly?
- Do the conclusions tie in with the original justification for the study and the research hypotheses?

? Final judgement:

- Has the psychological importance of the study been established?
- Did it achieve any progress with the topic matter?
- Is the study a competent piece of research considered overall relative to the declared (or emergent) objectives?
- In your judgement, was this worth publishing?

When writing a critique, you do not need to cover every aspect of the JARGON? scheme, as relevant issues depend on the article at hand. Some of the topics included in JARGON? may not apply to every paper. You should not try to shoehorn comments in so as to include each of the letters in JARGON? That would show a lack of selectivity. How many issues to raise depends on each particular article, but as a guideline, aim for five to seven issues for a critique. You can include more if warranted, but you do not want to make your critique too dense. It should be a high-level overview of the issues raised by a particular article. The JARGON? scheme is simply there to give you some tips on issues you may like to include in your critique. You need to decide how many issues to include and you start your critique with the most important one. JARGON? is not a recipe, so you would not start with justification, go on to appropriate or ambitious, then replicability and so on. That again would show a lack of selectivity.

A critique is *not* a summary of the paper. You should avoid adopting a passive acceptance or non-critical summary style of writing. Copying out parts of an article and presenting it as a critique is plagiarism. Selecting some important issues but without evaluating them is not a critique, it is a selective summary, which is to be avoided. You must evaluate, evaluate, evaluate!

Another style to avoid is the hypercritic or nit-picker. A 'critique' that simply consists of a list of complaints shows a lack of selectivity and balance. There is always some merit to be found, or the article would not have been published.

Equally, avoid making generic comments or raising vague issues that could be applied to any paper. Comments should be tied to specific issues raised in the particular article at hand.

Finally, a critique should be structured. Avoid a spaghetti style of writing or a shopping list by just itemising strengths and weakness in any old order as they occur. A critique should present a flowing argument illustrated with specific examples.

A critique should start with an introduction – not just a re-statement of the title or abstract; introduce the article and your critique of it. Highlight the points you will raise. It should also end with a conclusion – sum up the main issues you have presented and include your final judgement. When writing, present your arguments in your own words; you can include quotes, but do so sparingly. Lengthy quotes make the critique disjointed and can make your arguments hard to follow. Your reader may wonder where the article ends and your critique begins.

An important point to make is the guidelines and the JARGON? scheme are not prescriptive: there are often no correct or incorrect, right or wrong, issues to include in a critique. You can of course be wrong if you make a factual error but, when you write a critique, you are expressing your opinion and the strength of your critique relies on the strengths of the arguments your raise, the importance of the issues you choose to highlight, your ability to identify what is important and what is trivial, and your ability to back up your arguments with evidence from the paper you are critiquing. If you are writing a critique, rather than just critiquing a paper for your own benefit and understanding, you need to think who it is you are writing it for. If you are writing it for a general audience, the old adage is to write it for 'the intelligent non-expert who hasn't read the article', whoever that may be.

I suggest 'the intelligent non-expert' is your friend: imagine you are explaining the points you have to make about an article to a friend to give them an idea whether it is worthwhile for they themselves to go and read that paper, or give them tips on strengths and pitfalls if they do. The 'hasn't read the article' aspect means you have to provide enough detail that the points you are raising are clear, so you define the important elements of the argument you are making. You should lead your reader by the hand and explain the points you wish to raise in enough detail (but not too much detail!). For example, you wouldn't say

'The authors provide insufficient background justification for their study', as your reader would not know how to assess what you have written. You would say something like, 'The authors cite three previous studies on motion perception in migraine and, while motion perception is relevant to the authors' own study, citing just three is a rather limited number. Moreover, one study used the motion seen in a cloud of dots radiating outwards, one used coherent motion where moving dots are displayed with stationary noise dots, while the third used the motion seen in rotating spirals. The authors themselves used the illusory motion seen in the motion after-effect, so the relevance of the background literature cited is unclear.' (If it is not obvious, that is a completely made-up scenario and no-one would have an Introduction like that!) Your reader, however, would appreciate the point you are making rather than wondering what it is you are referring to by using the word 'insufficient'.

Another example, starting a critique with a comment that the sample size used in a study is rather small may be true, but it is hardly the most important observation you will have to make on the article and shows poor judgement on your part. Equally, just going through the article section by section as if you were summarising it and throwing comments in as you go along is not a good way to construct a critique, however valid the comments that you are making. The skill in writing a critique lies in selecting and prioritising what you will include and in what order. You will have to leave things out, so you have to decide which of the comments you make about the paper are worth mentioning and which can be left aside.

A critique should always begin with the most important issues you have to raise. Starting your critique by stating that some of the conclusions drawn are unwarranted because the relevant analyses have not been performed; or that the work constitutes a pioneering breakthrough in a particular field with the use of a new methodology; or that flaws in the method render the data questionable; or that an age-old question has been illuminated by coming at it from a novel angle, would provide a much better introduction than detailing minor points such as sample size (even if the minor points are true).

Remember that a critique is the writer's opinion, and that opinion must be backed up with evidence from the article being critiqued. You need to write to persuade *your* reader of the points you are making.

7 The brief general critique: example selection of issues

Kowalski, C. M., Kwiatkowska, K., Kwiatkowska, M. M., Poniklewska, K., Rogoza, R., & Schermer, J. A. (2018). The Dark Triad traits and intelligence: Machiavellians are bright, and narcissists and psychopaths are ordinary. *Personality and Individual Differences*, *135*, 1–6. https://doi.org/10.1016/j. paid.2018.06.049.

This chapter presents a selection of issues that students have raised in small group discussions when asked to start constructing a critique using the JAR-GON? scheme. These are provided to give you a glimpse into other people's judgement of this paper and what they have made of the guidance provided in class (the bulk of which is in Chapters 2 and 4 for this article). Perhaps have a go yourself at the JARGON? scheme before reading this chapter?

JARGON?

Justification: has a case been made for conducting the research? The consensus was that yes, a case has been made for conducting the research as there did not appear to be prior research in this area (the relationship between *fluid* intelligence and the dark triad personalities), so the rationale for the study was sound. The class recognised the null predictions were not appropriate, but commented that at least there was one hypothesis that was directional (Machiavellians would have higher scores than narcissists or psychopaths on a measure of fluid intelligence). Some thought the 'evil genius' hypothesis could have been explained better. Questions were raised regarding the level of detail to provide, so they were reminded to write for the intelligent non-expert who hasn't read the paper: describe the justification in enough detail and then evaluate its plausibility.

Appropriate or ambitious? Can the research question be addressed with the particular method and design adopted? (i.e. no particulars on how the design is implemented yet, just consider whether the hypotheses could be answered with a design of the sort proposed).

Various responses were provided to answer this issue, the foremost being that it was an appropriate design but conducted ambitiously. Good examples included the fact that there was no time limit on completing Raven's progressive matrices, which they suggested meant its reliability was undermined. The class suggested that there may be a lack of motivation or enticement for dark types, which means you can never be sure they are really trying – what is in it for them? The limited age range, the actual age (high teens) and the preponderance of females were highlighted as particular problems for the study. Some considered the sample size to be too small. The short dark triad and Raven's progressive matrices were considered appropriate as tools, but the way they were administered in a large classroom was considered problematic.

Replicability: has sufficient detail been provided for someone else to repeat the study? There was consensus that there was insufficient detail of what was actually done on the day in the testing room. They also mentioned the students had to complete other tests that were part of a battery in the first session, but the authors did not mention what they were, or how long they took to complete. The authors did not mention who was in the room to administer either the questionnaires or Raven's progressive matrices (was it their usual teacher or school psychologist?). They also wondered what happened during and after completing Raven's progressive matrices: was it possible to see other students' papers? Did the students just sit there after completion, or could they leave?

Generalisability:

- **Adequate measures (conceptual vs. operational): do the measures chosen adequately measure what they are supposed to?** The class thought that both the short dark triad questionnaire and Raven's progressive matrices were well validated measures, so they should be able to measure what they are supposed to; however, their implementation undermined their potential to do so.
- **Internal validity: is the internal logic of the research (design) satisfactory? Have the results been analysed correctly/thoroughly?** This question caused a little hesitation, but eventually the class thought that the analysis was flawed. They were less forthcoming with why it was flawed but eventually said there were too many comparisons in the structural equation model and it was not clearly explained. (This was probably the first time they had come across a structural equation model presented in this form.) They considered the extra t-tests comparing the traits were unnecessary.

  They suggested that good reliable measures cannot work miracles if the sample is wrong: teenagers may not yet show full dark triad traits or they may show them to be artificially high because of immaturity, in which case the measures will fail to do their job. They felt the report showed poor scientific rigour, as the authors do not give enough detail of the procedure, such as the time between the two sessions, how and where students were seated, what students who finished Raven's progressive matrices early did for half an hour, or how long the first session lasted.

- **External validity: how far can the results be generalised?** There was general agreement that generalisability was very low because they tested teenagers, and there was a preponderance of female students whereas, when dark traits exist, they are mostly exhibited by older males. The class considered that it was problematic to administer Raven's progressive matrices incorrectly, as there was no time limit, and this reduced the external validity of the study.

Organisation:

- **Have the authors presented their study in a well-organised, clear way and in sufficient detail?**
- **Are there serious flaws in the organisation or presentation of the paper (e.g. language, format, tables or graphs)?**
- **Is the article complete? Are all relevant sections provided?**

The class repeated that the structural equation model was complex and that it could have been explained in more detail. For example, they wondered how the coefficients were arrived at. Some discussed the positioning of the table and figures on the page after the discussion that relates to them, so it was pointed out that, although it is annoying when you have to flip back and forth between pages to match the text with a figure or a table, positioning is often in the hands of the publisher, not the authors. Of more importance is whether the graphs and table were themselves informative. They agreed that, for this article, the figures were more informative than the text at showing skew and outliers.

Overall, they thought the presentation and language were clear. They were prompted to consider whether the character descriptions of the three traits (a cartoon, an historical figure in Vlad the Impaler, and the Unabomber) were adequately scientific. Were there no other examples they could have drawn upon?

iNterpretation:

- **Have the data and analyses been interpreted satisfactorily/correctly?**
- **Do the conclusions tie in with the original justification for the study and the research hypotheses?**

The consensus here was that the results were not discussed particularly well. The authors overstated their findings and there were some overgeneralised comments. One group considered it poor to use words like 'evil genius' when referring to school children. The class agreed that support for the 'evil genius' hypothesis did not follow from their design, the data collected or the analyses performed.

The class was concerned that the authors did not discuss the small amount of variance accounted for by the structural equation model ($R^2 = 0.05$), they just went straight back into discussing the evil genius hypothesis. One group suggested that, because they had only one main hypothesis about Machiavellians, they had hamstrung themselves by what conclusions they could draw at the end. The authors' discussion was general rather than tied to the results obtained. They added that the authors just repeated the Introduction for a large part of the Discussion.

? Final judgement:

- **Has the psychological importance of the study been established?**
- **Did it achieve any progress with the topic matter?**
- **Is the study a competent piece of research considered overall relative to the declared (or emergent) objectives?**
- **In your judgement, was this worth publishing?**

The overall view was that this was an interesting area of study, but this particular article lacked scientific rigour. The class thought there were grounds for looking at fluid intelligence and personality traits. Since the results were consistent with the hypotheses, some thought that progress has been made even if the generalisability was very limited. They appreciated that the authors had noted some of the limitations in their work. However, the design was flawed, and there were problems with replicability and generalisability. Some were undecided whether it was worth publishing. Some thought they would send it back for a revision, others thought that if it were their choice, they would reject it.

Others were more damning; they considered a fatal flaw was the lack of generalisability and that it therefore did not advance our understanding of the area. They conceded that this article may inspire others to do a better version, but considered this article did not deliver much beyond finding that fluid intelligence may be a factor with these personality traits, or at least with Machiavellians. They thought that both fluid and crystallised intelligence should have been assessed and their association with the dark triad traits: if they had found a double dissociation, then they would have been able to conclude something about fluid intelligence differences between the three groups. Others picked up on the small R^2 and concluded that this study did not really contribute anything if their model explained so little variance in the underlying data. They thought the additional t-tests appeared to be the authors grasping at straws.

Order of points for a critique

As has been mentioned, there is no right or wrong order of the points raised in your critique, so long as you can explain what you are discussing and why it is important to do so. Here are some suggestions for the ordering of points from different students:

1 Generalisability, flawed procedure, replicability, interpretation, ending with positive points, e.g. that it was an interesting area, and the justification was fair, then a final judgement.

2 Good justification (looking at fluid intelligence), inappropriate sample (too young and predominantly female), some irrelevant analyses, missing information on the test sessions and procedure, concerns about experimenter effects (who administered the tests), inability to replicate, ending with comments on predicting a null hypothesis and a final judgement.

3 Generalisability, justification, appropriate or ambitious, replicability, interpretation, final judgement.

4 Generalisability, justification, replicability, interpretation, organisation, appropriate or ambitious, final judgement.

5 Organisation, appropriate or ambitious, generalisability, interpretation, justification, replicability, final judgement.

6 Appropriate or ambitious, generalisability, justification, replicability, organisation, interpretation, final judgement.

As mentioned before, there is no right or wrong structure to a critique, it is your judgement. Each of these orderings is completely acceptable, so long as the comments made about each issue are presented clearly and the critique as a whole is balanced (finding strengths as well as weaknesses).

8 An example critique

The course this book is based on runs like a journal club each week: we discuss particular articles in small groups. All of the articles presented so far have been discussed in class and, previously, used for the exam. The details of the articles only are distributed the weekend before the exam and then, on the day, the students have three hours to answer two set questions (the exercises that have appeared at the end of each article in Chapters 3–5) and then write a critique. Here is an example of one of them. Perhaps have a go yourself before reading this chapter?

Simor, P., Köteles, F., Sándor, P., Petke, Z., & Bódizs, R. (2011). Mindfulness and dream quality: The inverse relationship between mindfulness and negative dream affect. *Scandinavian Journal of Psychology*, 52(4), 369–375. https://doi.org/ 10.1111/j.1467-9450.2011.00888.x.

Q1: In the justification for their study, do the authors successfully weave together their discussion of mindfulness, sleep quality, cognitive behaviour therapy for insomnia, nightmares, waking well-being and psychopathological conditions? Is their suggestion of protective factors overcoming dream disturbances thereby plausible? How many hypotheses were presented? Evaluate the measures used and their appropriateness to address their research hypotheses.

In this article by Simor *et al.* (2011), the authors investigate the relationship between mindfulness and dream disturbances. The authors satisfactorily provide the reader with an overview of existing research indicating the beneficial effects of mindfulness on factors such as emotional states, self-regulatory capacities and sleep quality. Given the relationship between psychopathological disorders and sleep disturbances, and a lack of research into the links between mindfulness and the emotional aspects of dreaming, their research aim is argued to be sufficiently justified. However, the execution of the research question definitely warrants improvement.

Mindfulness is accurately conceptualised as a mental state of awareness that acts on the contents of consciousness as opposed to existing within them. The authors highlight the importance of self-regulation and successful stress management for promoting well-being and in determining the reactions to and the recovery times from adverse life experiences. Additionally, various psychopathological conditions are underpinned by impaired self-regulation and stress management strategies and are associated with dream disturbances and poor sleep quality. The extant literature cited within the paper suggests that mindfulness promotes improvements in sleep quality, positive affect, self-regulation and stress reduction.

In light of the presentation of this information in the Introduction, it is concluded that mindfulness does present itself as a potential protective factor against dream disturbances. This is due to its effects on individuals' regulatory capacities and cognitive flexibility, which are argued to influence sleep quality and more specifically the emotional quality of dreams. This suggestion by the authors is further strengthened by research that suggests mindfulness is a skill that can be learned and would thus be a viable alternative to the medicalisation of sleep and psychopathological disorders. However, the reasoning behind the authors' presentation of mindfulness coupled with cognitive behavioural therapy (CBT) as a treatment for insomnia is not made explicitly clear. Perhaps it stems from an understanding of the increased self-awareness of physiology, psychology and behaviour associated with mindfulness, which could be argued is similar to the key principle of CBT.

Eleven hypotheses are clearly stated by the authors in their Introduction, although some of them are grouped together under one general hypothesis and a further 4 comparisons were made which were not specified (see the hypotheses list at the end of this answer). An additional hypothesis regarding gender differences was tested for in the first two regression analyses despite not being pre-specified. The effects of this variable were only discussed in the Discussion and not in the Introduction.

As a preliminary investigation into this novel research area, it is argued that the measures and design used were appropriate for addressing the authors' research hypothesis. Their main objective was to investigate the relationship between mindfulness and two measures of dream disturbances. The study was a within-subject, cross-sectional questionnaire-based design and is suitable to the aims of the researchers to explore the associations between measurements of the variables. The various questionnaires used were all previously validated as being effective measures of the variables in question (trait anxiety, perceived stress, trait mindfulness, dream anxiety and negative dream quality). The reliability of these variables was also verified with the use of Cronbach's alpha and was found to be acceptable for all variables except one, which was given a moderate measure of internal consistency. Although measurements for control variables, previously shown to have an association with sleep quality, were obtained, it is argued that there are many more important variables that were omitted from the discussion of the rationale and the design of the study. For instance, the use of drugs, alcohol, prescription medicines, diet and patterns of technology use have all been shown to affect sleep quality. Had these variables been accounted for and incorporated into the design and analysis of the study, it would have enabled the authors to draw stronger conclusions about the predictive value of their investigated variables.

In summary, although a satisfactory rationale for the study in question has been provided by the authors, it is argued that the failure to address and incorporate the effects of other potential predictor variables into the study's design and therefore analysis has limited the potential value of this research into a novel area of interest.

Hypotheses list

- That there will be a positive correlation between both levels of disturbed dreaming (negative dream quality and dream anxiety) and levels of trait anxiety and perceived stress (4).
- Mindfulness, on the other hand, will be negatively correlated with levels of trait anxiety and perceived stress (2) and with both levels of disturbed dreaming (negative dream quality and dream anxiety) (2).
- Mindfulness will be associated with less severe dream disturbances by moderating the effect of trait anxiety on dream disturbances. This will be reflected in an interaction between mindfulness and anxiety and their association with both levels of dream disturbances (2).
- Mindfulness will moderate the relationship between negative dream quality and dream state anxiety (1).
- In Table 1, which displays the descriptive statistics and the results of Kendall's tau test, an additional two associations are tested: that between dream anxiety and negative dream quality (1), and between trait anxiety and perceived stress (1).
- Predictive value of gender on negative dream quality and dream anxiety (2).

Q2: Are the data presented clearly? Which analyses were used and were all of them necessary? Is the introduction of gender into the analyses justified, or the interaction term between STAIT and MAAS when each were also entered separately into the analyses? Comment on the conclusions that were drawn. In research like this, would it be useful to control for previous experience in meditation, mindfulness or yoga training?

The paper by Simor *et al.* (2011) presents the findings of a study of the associations between mindfulness and two measures of dream disturbances. Despite the addition of a previously unspecified variable (gender), the statistical analyses are clearly laid out and the conclusions drawn are satisfactorily related back to their hypotheses. However, some aspects of the output from the regression analyses were omitted and had to be worked out by hand. Additionally, although interpretations drawn by the authors are backed by statistically significant findings, it is argued that they are limited by a failure to account for the effects of other variables previously established as being associated with sleep quality.

Primarily, the authors report that the distribution of the data was analysed for normality and that the data were not normally distributed. Kendall's tau test for correlation was subsequently conducted, as it is a non-parametric test that tests for associations between ordinal data, of which all the measurements taken were. The results of these tests were clearly presented in Table 1 and produced findings that validated all of the predictions of hypothesis 1.

Three hierarchical linear regressions were appropriately used to test the remaining three hypotheses. In order to assess the independent predictive power of mindfulness (and its interaction with trait anxiety) on dream disturbances after controlling for the predictive value of gender, perceived stress and trait anxiety, the use of hierarchical regression is suitable. This model of regression allows the various predictor variables to be input into the model in a predetermined order on the basis of their pre-established significant association to the dependent variable. However, the authors do not say why they entered the variables in the order reported.

In the first regression analysis, dream quality was the dependent variable. Gender, perceived stress, trait anxiety, mindfulness and the interaction between mindfulness and trait anxiety were entered in separate steps. The same model was used for the second regression analysis, except that the dependent variable was dream anxiety. For the third regression analysis, the dependent variable was again dream anxiety, and dream quality, mindfulness and their interaction were entered in separate steps. The only significant contribution made by the interaction was for the second regression. For the first regression, gender, trait anxiety and mindfulness predicted dream quality. For the second, gender, trait anxiety, mindfulness and the interaction term between mindfulness and trait anxiety predicted dream anxiety. For the third, dream quality and mindfulness predicted dream anxiety.

By incorporating mindfulness into the model towards the end of each analysis, after having analysed the predictive value of the aforementioned three variables, the authors were able to disambiguate its predictive power. The interaction term was subsequently introduced into the regression model to achieve the same outcome, although it did not add anything significant for the first regression. Due to the variables input prior to mindfulness having been shown to be associated with dream quality, this method of analysis was justified. However, there was no previous mention of gender differences with respect to mindfulness or prevalence of psychological imbalances or impaired sleep patterns. Despite mention in the Discussion of gender differences in the affective qualities of dreaming, its addition as the primary variable in the equation is not justified. On the other hand, the previously mentioned incorporation of the interaction term was justified and necessary to understand whether there was an interactive effect of mindfulness and trait anxiety on dream disturbances as predicted in hypothesis 3. However, there is not sufficient mention of how they produced the interaction term. Thus, it is not possible to assess whether this measurement was representative of the interaction that the authors sought to examine.

The results of the regression analyses were clearly presented, although there was no mention of the R^2 value for any of the regression equations except for the first addition of gender. Nevertheless, the ΔR^2 values did enable this to be worked out by hand. The five explanatory variables accounted for 14.8% of the variance in dream disturbances in each of the final regression equations for the two measures of the dependent variable (the first two regression analyses). There was no mention of these values anywhere in the paper, which to me suggests the authors were not confident that they would strongly support the conclusions drawn. The main conclusion drawn by the authors is that their study has shown mindfulness predicts reduced sleep disturbances and thus may be a protective factor against them. Statistically they have produced findings which show that increased mindfulness significantly predicts reductions in dream disturbances. However, given the little variation in negative dream quality (1.2%) and dream anxiety (3.1%) explained by the addition of mindfulness to the two regression equations, the strength of this claim is questionable.

To control for previous experience with mindfulness or other forms of training that similarly improve self-awareness and cognitive flexibility seems excessive, as this study only sought to examine the associations of trait mindfulness with dream disturbances. The incorporation of these variables would be of more use in future research. For example, an experimental study investigating the effects of a mindfulness-based training on sleep quality could control for these variables and use a between-subject design with a control group and an intervention group divided on the basis of whether you have previous experience in practices that increase mindfulness. This would allow researchers to examine the relative contribution of the different variables on any observed effects.

In summary, despite the omission of the total variance explained by the regression models, the authors have clearly presented the findings of their study. They have drawn conclusions that are supported by the statistically significant findings. However, given the relatively little variance explained by their models of regression, their conclusions are not a fair representation of what they have actually observed in their study.

Q3: Write a brief general critique of the report.

Simor *et al.* (2011) report the findings of a study that explored the relationship between trait mindfulness and two measurements of dream disturbances in a sample of 587 undergraduate students. They found a negative association between the variables, i.e. that increased mindfulness predicts reduced dream disturbances (dream anxiety and negative dream quality). Additionally, the results revealed that trait mindfulness may moderate the detrimental influence of trait anxiety on dream anxiety but not negative dream quality. This critique will explore how, despite the statistically significant findings, they were still relatively weak and thus not very meaningful. Additionally, there are various methodological limitations that also restrict the validity of the authors' conclusions. Findings of significance that may potentially emerge from this novel area of research have important implications for the treatment of psychopathological disorders and for general physical and psychological well-being. Therefore, future research needs to address the limitations of the research paper in question and produce a more comprehensive study to examine the predictive value of mindfulness for sleep disturbances.

Within their Introduction, the authors accurately conceptualise mindfulness and highlight the various relationships it has with self-regulation, indices of mental health and sleep quality. Dream disturbances, characterised by negative dream quality and waking dream anxiety, have been linked with psychopathologies and theorised to be underpinned by poor emotional self-regulation. As mindfulness is known to increase self-regulatory capacities, the claim that this may in turn affect dream disturbances is justified as being a novel area of research. One of the most important aspects of designing a study is to ensure the planning and acquisition of data account for as many additional variables that could potentially explain any variation in the dependent variable. The use of hierarchical linear regression to enter variables with previously established associations with sleep into the equation step by step did enable the researchers to establish the independent predictive value of mindfulness. However, the authors failed to collect sufficient information regarding other potentially explanatory variables. For instance, the sample group are all undergraduate students who are renowned for engaging in excessive drinking, drug-taking and unhealthy eating. All of these factors have known detrimental influences on sleep quality. If these factors had been incorporated into the analysis, perhaps the explanatory power of mindfulness would be different. Additionally, any observed relationship between mindfulness and sleep disturbances would have been strengthened by the increased internal validity of the design resulting from a reduction in the possibility of an omitted variable bias.

In addition to collecting data reflecting all possible predictor variables, care must be taken to ensure that the selected measurements are accurate reflections of the independent and dependent variables. Although the authors used measurements that had been previously validated, there was no information provided about the time period that items in the questionnaires were supposedly measuring except for items within the perceived stress scale. This is especially relevant for the two dependent variables (dream anxiety and negative dream quality). The accuracy of the dream recall would likely have been adversely affected with each day that passed from the actual dream experience. Additionally, the disposition of the participants likely played a part on their appraisal and thus their perception of the quality of their dream and any dream-induced emotional states. As an individual's self-regulatory capacities have been hypothesised to affect dream disturbances, it is assumed that it will affect the emotional valence attributed to a specific experience. In order to ensure the accurate measurement of the dependent variables, future research should employ more objectively verifiable measurements of dream disturbances. To the credit of the authors, this limitation is partially raised, and they suggest the use of dream logs in the future. However, I would argue that this was still a large oversight on the part of the researchers and that stronger suggestions could be made. For example, if a similar study was conducted in a sleep lab where levels of physiological arousal were measured in addition to a dream log noting the timings of sleep disturbances, this would be a very reliable measurement and would subsequently strengthen any observed findings.

The strength of the current research paper resides in the novelty of the research area. Psychopathological conditions place a huge toll on the afflicted individuals, their loved ones and society at large. Currently, pharmacological treatments are the dominant treatment for most issues of mental health. Although in some cases they are effective, they mostly serve to address expressed symptoms as opposed to underlying causes. Many of these disorders are underpinned by impaired self-regulation and negative cognitions that arise in response to a dynamic interplay of genetic predispositions and early life experience. As mindfulness has been shown to be a skill that can be learned to improve self-regulation, cognitive flexibility and sleep quality, it could be a treatment option that improves the causal cognitions and neurophysiology of mental health disorders. If the results of this study can be replicated with a higher degree of statistical significance and strength, then mindfulness as predicted by the authors may represent a potential protective factor to dream disturbances and have wider implications for treatment too.

Another aspect of the sample that warrants improvement is the sampling. The participants were opportunistically sampled and were all undergraduate students. Additionally, men were overrepresented in the study (72.4% males, 27.6% females). The authors do acknowledge this limitation somewhat and state their results can only be generalised to healthy students. However, this does not account for the fact that the predictive value of mindfulness for dream disturbances in female students may have been systematically under- or over-estimated. Erring on the side of caution, it should be advised that the findings are only applicable to male students instead. The recommendation of the authors to conduct the study with other groups such as clinical populations is a valid point. If this relationship was explored in an intervention-based study with a sample from a clinical population and a more representative control group, the protective and therapeutic effects of mindfulness could be further evaluated with increased validity.

To conclude, the article by Simor *et al.* (2011) provides the findings of a study exploring a novel research area. The results suggest that mindfulness significantly predicts reductions in dream disturbances. Also, in alignment with the continuity hypothesis of dreaming, mindfulness may potentially moderate the adverse effects of trait anxiety on dream quality perhaps by improving emotional regulation. Although there were some significant findings, the explanatory power of mindfulness was low. Additionally, given that the authors failed to control for other variables that could have potentially explained some of the variance in their models, it is argued that the conclusions drawn were a misrepresentation of the actual meaning of their results and should be approached with caution until more comprehensive studies are conducted. This does not negate the contribution of the research to the ongoing study of mindfulness, sleep, dreaming and non-pharmaceutical-based treatments of mental health disorders by opening up a new area of research. However, until the limitations are addressed, and the results replicated in different populations, further research is certainly necessary.

9 Overview and conclusions

The general aims of the book have been to: (1) encourage critical reading and analysis of psychological research reports; (2) show how design principles and statistics are applied in psychological research; and (3) consider the psychological importance of published research studies. Through the ten general questions (10GQs) and JARGON? scheme, it has provided guidance on how to review articles comprehensively, evaluate the justification, method, analysis and interpretation, and ultimately construct a stand-alone critique. The intention has been to make you an active – rather than a passive – reader of scientific articles, as well as provide you with skills applicable when you come to conduct your own research.

Throughout, there has been an emphasis on linking sections, considering the article as a WHOLE so that, for example, the method and variables selected are related back to hypotheses, the analyses performed are related back to the method, selected variables and hypotheses, and the conclusions drawn are related back to all four. The articles cited have covered research that falls within what could be termed the mainstream experimental research tradition in Psychology, where there are independent variables (selected by the researcher) and dependent variables (the data that have been collected). See Chapter 3 and the articles by Yeh *et al.* (2017) and Blaesi and Wilson (2010). It has also covered research that has looked for relationships in the data, using correlation, principal components analysis, structural equation modelling, MANOVA, ANOVA and hierarchical regression. See Chapters 4 and 5 and the articles by Simor *et al.* (2011), Rauthmann and Kolar (2013) and Kowalski *et al.* (2018).

The book revolves around critical evaluation using two simple learning aids that can be applied to all research articles: the 10GQs and the JARGON? scheme. These learning aids are not presented as recipes, rather, they are tools to help you identify the strengths and weaknesses in published research articles, prioritise them, and construct an overall critical assessment. This is a crucial difference to other texts in this area: those that do offer critiques of articles provide comments relevant to that particular article, they do not provide an overarching framework that can be applied to any research article.

So, while the examples in this book have been mainstream experimental research, the principles behind the 10GQs and JARGON? are applicable to other types of research. It is not a difficult stretch to appreciate that they are relevant for electrophysiological (EP, ERP) and imaging (fMRI, MEG)[1] research. Each of these techniques begins with the design of an experiment to be completed while participants are being recorded or scanned. A commentary on analysing electrophysiological or imaging data has not been included, but the design of the experiments that use these recording or scanning tools is amenable to the analytic approach described here. The inclusion of electrophysiological or imaging measurements may constrain the design of the experiment and the selection of tasks particularly for imaging where overt responses are difficult to incorporate, as the act of responding will activate brain regions associated with that response rather than the region of interest. Electrophysiological studies hand in hand with a behavioural task are less constrained, physically (the participant is not lying in a tube, for example), but care in the type of response and how that translates into unwanted EEG potentials is the same. Often the observer makes no response in electrophysiological and imaging studies, yet the discussion of issues raised on justification, method and design are equally applicable, regardless of the mode of response, or the absence of a response.

Much clinical research is also amenable to analysis with the 10GQs and the JARGON? scheme. Many researchers run standard experiments on a clinical and a non-clinical control group which, other than being unable to randomly allocate participants to the two conditions, attracts the same issues as a standard experiment. That participants cannot be randomly allocated to groups makes these types of studies quasi-experiments rather than true experiments. For example, the performance of a migraine group can be compared with that of a headache-free control group on various tasks to try to understand the differences between those with and without the condition (Shepherd, 2006; Tibber et al., 2014; Shepherd & Patterson, 2020). Equally, the performance of participants with anxiety can compared with that of participants without anxiety on different tasks (Van Dam, Earleywine & Altarriba, 2012), or the performance of children with autism can be compared with that of intellectually matched control children, again on particular tasks (Ropar, Mitchell & Ackroyd, 2003). The list can go on and on: those interested in depression, schizophrenia, epilepsy, post-traumatic stress, spider phobia, insomnia, dyslexia – there is a myriad of quasi-experiments depending on the clinical group of interest.

All these research endeavours try to determine what the underlying differences are between people with or without the condition (other than the fact that they have a severe headache, or are anxious, or have a diagnosis of autism, and so on), mostly with the aim of ultimately developing better treatment or management strategies. The skill with quasi-experiments and clinical groups is to choose tasks that are capable of showing group differences, and in a way that sheds light on aspects of that condition. The best approach is to take something that is reasonably well understood (e.g. motion perception – we know a great deal about how and where motion is processed in the brain) and apply it to something that is poorly understood (e.g. migraine, anxiety, depression, autism). If there is a model of what differs between people with and without that condition (such as whether the cortex is hyperexcitable in migraine, or is it hypoexcitable? (Shepherd, 2007)), then tasks can be selected where clear predictions from alternate models are possible. In that way, depending on the results, there is support for one or other model and theory is advanced, ultimately with implications for treatment.

Most of the components of JARGON? and some of the 10GQs are also applicable to qualitative research. There is already a wide range of criteria directed at diverse audiences for assessing the quality of qualitative research. For instance, broad evaluative criteria exist for funding bodies, journal editors and reviewers, such as the recently developed APA guidelines by Levitt *et al.* (2018), or examples of researchers from psychology and associated disciplines evaluating their own research (e.g. Finlay, 2011; Yardley, 2008). In addition, due to the pluralistic nature of qualitative research in terms of epistemological traditions, objectives and methods, some qualitative approaches such as Interpretative Phenomenological Analysis (IPA) and Discourse Analysis have developed specific sets of criteria (O'Reilly *et al.*, 2020; Smith, Bekker & Cheater, 2011; Nizza, Farr & Smith, 2021).

Each of these sets of criteria is useful after learning the basics of qualitative research and, in particular, IPA. They are especially useful as knowledge of, and skill with doing, qualitative research develop. The 10GQs and the JARGON? scheme are a useful starting point if you are more familiar with evaluating quantitative rather than qualitative research. This is because, although researchers require a different mindset and language when carrying out qualitative research, it remains the case that similar quality markers can be applied to both types of research, including methodological coherence, ethical issues and transparency.

Both the 10GQs and JARGON? can be adapted and used with qualitative research to organise thinking and to generate material for a critical review. The basic structure, logic and purpose are the same for both forms of research.

The 10GQs

Q1a: What is the paper about? (Does the report formulate a specific research question not previously addressed? If so, what is it? If not, can you glean the aims/objectives of the study?)

Q1b: Have the authors made a compelling case for addressing their particular topic? (Do the background and rationale for the study persuade you it is worth doing and that it will generate something new?)

Q2: Have the authors made a compelling case for their way of handling the topic? (Is there a good fit between the theoretical/epistemological underpinnings of the qualitative approach used and the research question?)

Q3: What is the design of the study? (Is there a full and clear explanation given of what participation involved? If not, what is missing?)

Q4a: Participant selection (on what basis were the participants selected?)

Q4b: What can be said about the sample? (Is there a sensible justification for the sample and sufficient information provided?)

Q5: How are the data analysed? This reflects a concern with technicalities and the process of analysis (transparency).

Q6: What are the main analytic findings? What is the outcome of the analysis?

Q7: What is the quality of the analysis? In your view, is it persuasive, plausible, credible?

Q8: Are the findings and their implications discussed in light of relevant literature?

Q9: What are the strengths of the report?

Q10: What are the limitations of the report?

There is a change in emphasis from the expected answers to the 10GQs for experimental and qualitative research. The qualitative questions are geared to asking what YOU think. You should use your answers to Q1–Q8 to help you answer Q9 and Q10.

JARGON?

Justification: what are the main arguments for the importance and relevance of doing the study? How well have the researchers made a case for the relevance/usefulness of the study?

Appropriate: is the appropriate approach used? Do the aims/objectives 'fit' with the research question, aims and objectives?

Replicability: has sufficient information been provided?

Generalisability: is it generalisable enough?

There are both differences and similarities between quantitative and qualitative research and some key differences are discussed briefly here. First, the small sample sizes typically used in qualitative studies mean that thinking about generalisation in statistical terms makes little sense. It is more appropriate to think about the study at hand and its theoretical generalisation – for example, how the interpretation of the thematic findings might be inferred to similar groups. Second, qualitative researchers assume an explicit reflexive stance towards their research. Reflexivity involves the researcher reflecting throughout the entire process on how they have shaped the research, which includes how research questions are developed, the interpretative engagement during the analysis, and how their professional experience, existing assumptions and knowledge influence the carrying out and outcome of studies. Third, many qualitative researchers aim for their findings to resonate with the reader, how they give the reader a better 'what-it-is-like' dimension of what is being studied. Often, a successful analysis of the data (e.g. interviews) is judged on how well the write-up of the research is in giving the reader detailed insight and appreciation of the topic being studied.

Organisation: what can you say about the organisation and presentation of the results?

iNterpretation: do the researchers interpret and make sense of their analysis?

? Final judgement: was the study worth doing?

In conclusion, the guidance and procedures presented in this book are aimed to make you think about every aspect of any research paper. Not all will be applicable to every paper you may read, but they are not meant to be sacrosanct entities. Instead, think of them as tools and pick and choose those elements that can help you with whatever it is you are reading, be it research articles, interviews, newspaper columns or books. The main thing to do is to think!

© Michael Leunig

Note

1 EP: evoked potential and ERP: event-related potential, both from an EEG: electroencephalogram; fMRI: functional magnetic resonance imaging; MEG: magnetoencephalography.

References

Finlay, L. (2011). *Phenomenology for Therapists: Researching the Lived World*. New York: Wiley.

Levitt, H. M., Bamberg, M., Creswell, J. W. *et al.* (2018). Journal article reporting standards for qualitative primary, qualitative meta-analytic, and mixed methods research in psychology: The APA Publications and Communications Board Task Force Report. *American Psychologist, 73*(1), 26–46. https://doi.org/10.1037/amp0000151.

Nizza, I. E., Farr, J., & Smith, J. A. (2021). Achieving excellence in interpretative phenomenological analysis (IPA): Four markers of high quality. *Qualitative Research in Psychology, 18*(3), 369–386. https://doi.org/10.1080/14780887.2020.1854404.

O'Reilly, M., Kiyimba, N., Lester, J. N. *et al.* (2020). Establishing quality in discursive psychology: Three domains to consider. *Qualitative Research in Psychology, 18*(3), 406–425. https://doi.org/10.1080/14780887.2020.1810373.

Ropar, D., Mitchell, P., & Ackroyd, K. (2003). Do children with autism find it difficult to offer alternative interpretations to ambiguous figures? *British Journal of Developmental Psychology, 21*(3), 387–395. https://doi.org/10.1348/026151003322277766.

Shepherd, A. J. (2006). Local and global motion after-effects are both enhanced in migraine, and the underlying mechanisms differ across cortical areas. *Brain, 129*(7), 1833–1843. https://doi.org/10.1093/brain/awl124.

Shepherd, A. J. (2007). Models of cortical function in migraine: Can psychophysical studies distinguish between them? A review of the evidence for interictal cortical hyper- and hypo-excitability, in L. B. Clarke (ed.) *Migraine Disorders Research Trends*. New York: Nova Science, pp. 145–164.

Shepherd, A. J., & Patterson, A. J. K. (2020). Exploration of anomalous perceptual experiences in migraine between attacks using the Cardiff Anomalous Perceptions Scale. *Consciousness and Cognition, 82*, 102945. https://doi.org/10.1016/j.concog.2020.102945.

Smith, J. A., Bekker, H., & Cheater, F. (2011). Theoretical versus pragmatic design in qualitative research. *Nurse Researcher, 18*(2), 39–51. https://doi.org/10.7748/nr2011.01.18.2.39.c8283.

Tibber, M. S., Kelly, M. G., Jansari, A. *et al.* (2014). An inability to exclude visual noise in migraine. *Investigative Ophthalmology and Visual Science, 55*(4), 2539–2546. https://doi.org/10.1167/iovs.14-13877.

Van Dam, N. T., Earleywine, M., & Altarriba, J. (2012). Anxiety attenuates awareness of emotional faces during rapid serial visual presentation. *Emotion, 12*(4), 796–806. https://doi.org/10.1037/a0024648.

Yardley, L. (2008). Demonstrating validity in qualitative psychology, in J. A. Smith (ed.) *Qualitative Psychology: A Practical Guide to Research Methods*, 2nd edn. London: Sage, pp. 235–251.

Index

Page numbers in italics are figures; with 't' are tables.